I'VE GOT A SONG TO WRITE

Kent Westberry's Story

60 Years in Country Music as a Songwriter,
Singer, Record Producer, and Entertainer

DORRANCE
PUBLISHING CO
EST. 1920
PITTSBURGH, PENNSYLVANIA 15238

Dorrance Publishing Co
585 Alpha Drive, Suite 103
Pittsburgh, PA 15238
Visit our website at *www.dorrancebookstore.com*

ISBN: 978-1-6480-4112-9
eISBN 978-1-6480-4919-4

FOREWORD

I would like to express my appreciation to all those who were associated in helping me put this book together. My daughters, Susan Thomsen Clark, Judy McClure, and Dawn Millis, helped with their love, typing skills, and technical knowledge. I thank my lovely wife, Dale Turner Westberry, for her inspiration and for providing so many memories that would probably still be forgotten without her. Special thanks also go to Hal and Donna Harbour for their invaluable assistance in overseeing and editing the content. I would also like to express my appreciation to my good friend and fellow songwriter, Wayne Gray, for helping with some of the stories he remembered.

You know, it's funny how it seems that no two people agree on exactly how a story happened. They see the same thing, yet later, recall it differently. I just want you to know that in this book I have tried to be totally honest in relating to you these experiences. I tell how they occurred in my life as seen through the eyes of the person who lived it – ME!!

My deepest thanks also go to all the musicians who worked with me in my bands, "The Memory Makers" and "The Chaperones." There's not enough space here to name them all. You know who you are. My thanks go also to Mel Tillis Jr. ("Sonny Boy"), who called recently to ask if I would mind if he called his band "The Memory Makers" since I have retired. I really appreciated that he asked for my blessing. He's a great talent and my good friend. I said, "Sure."

Chapter 1

HERE COMES THE ROCKER

I first saw the light of day on May 23rd, 1939, in Jackson Memorial Hospital in Miami, Florida. I had two very loving parents who were overjoyed at my arrival. So was I! I had a normal childhood growing up. Yep, I was the only child. Normal? Well, that's open to debate.

Mom and Dad were very good dancers and liked ballroom dancing. They loved big band music. My mom was even a professional tap dancer for a while, but then she quit to take care of me. She was born in Aberdeen, South Dakota, and settled in Miami with her sister, Marie. That's where she met Dad – later, of course. My mother had a ukulele she used to play. She taught me a few chords. I would sit outside on the front porch and sing as loud as I could.

My dad worked for Eastern Airlines. Later he sold used cars. He was always a hard worker - I never saw him without a job. He was born in Valdosta, Georgia, but grew up in Miami, Florida. He was next-to-youngest in a family of six brothers and one sister. He always had a funny philosophy and a great sense of humor. He told me once that to go on a picnic, all you have to do is spread a blanket on an ant hill in your front yard, turn on the garden hose, sprinkle sand in your sandwiches, and you've got a picnic at the beach. I still recall other words of wisdom he lived by: "Let it rain, let it shine; if I get wet, it's my behind."

I can remember, when I was six years old, tuning in a country music station on the radio and loving what I heard. The radio guy's name was "Smilin' Sammy" Fife, and there was a girl who yodeled. I was smitten!

When I was about nine or ten, a buddy and I went to Baker's Haulover Beach in Miami one afternoon, and the tide was out. There were sandbars and you could walk way out there. We walked about half a block from shore until I realized the water was up to my knees. The tide was coming in.

I started walking toward shore. It was getting deeper, and I could see I couldn't swim that far, but I kept walking until it was chest-high and rising. It got up past my chin, and I was still about twenty yards from shore. I couldn't breathe. I felt a numbness in my head - it was like my life flashed before me in seconds. I thought I was drowning.

All of a sudden there was a man who stood beside me. He asked if I was all right. I shook my head "NO!" He grabbed me by the hair on my head, pulled me up, and put me where I could touch bottom. Then he just disappeared. Looking back now, I honestly believe he was an angel.

I remember when I was about ten or eleven, about 1949 or so, there was a movie playing in downtown Miami called *Hollywood Barn Dance* starring Ernest Tubb, the famous singer. It was about Ernest growing up on a farm, then putting a band together and hitting the road. Mom took me to see it. I loved it! I've still got a copy of it.

The Bare Facts: When I was thirteen or so, a couple of buddies and I spent one summer hanging around Coconut Grove Marina on Coconut Grove Bay, where people would come in and dock their boats. We were exploring the water's edge when we saw the outline of a boat sunk in about three feet of water. We pulled it up on shore. It was about fifteen feet long and had a hole about the size of a softball right in the middle of it. We went and got some tar, sealed it up, and named it *Long John*. We got a couple of oars and rowed out into the channel quite a ways from shore.

There were a lot of little islands out there. We used to row out to them and spend the day. We had to take a big can with us to keep bailing water out of the boat because it kept leaking. About every hour the boat would fill up to about a quarter full. One particular day we were skinny-dippin' (buck naked) in the channel. Our clothes were in the boat. All of a sudden, here comes this small yacht full of girls. They stopped and cut off their motor. Then they all started laughing and hootin' and hollerin' and pointing at us! We were stuck in the water for about an hour before they left. We finally were able to retrieve our clothes. So much for girls!

I grew up playing sports, particularly baseball. I had a baseball uniform that I proudly wore when I played in the neighborhood with the other kids, even though it was one hundred percent wool and it itched - especially in the Florida heat! But I wore it anyway. One day I traded my uniform to the kid next door for an old guitar I didn't know how to play. I eventually taught myself to play it.

Take Me where the Flowers Grow: When I was fourteen or fifteen, I decided I wanted to sing songs that I hadn't heard on the radio before. I started writing my own songs. I remember that the first song I ever wrote was "Back in Virginia where the Bluebonnets Grow." My dad got the biggest kick out of that. He said, "How does he know bluebonnets grow in Virginia? He's never been out of Florida!"

We moved again, this time right across the street from the Boy's Club of Miami. I loved it! I spent most every day over there, playing sports and games like pool and ping-pong and such. Tommy Greenaway was a guy who worked there. He was a couple of years older than I was. Tommy was a senior at Coral Gables High School. I was a sophomore. We became great friends and hung out together. When Tommy graduated he went into the Navy. I didn't see him for a long time after that.

A Mouth full of Baseball: One afternoon I was playing baseball and pitching. I threw a fastball, and the batter smashed a line drive right

3

into my mouth - I didn't even see it coming! It knocked my two front teeth out of their sockets and busted my top lip open. They took me to the hospital and sewed up my lip, then to a dental specialist who filed my teeth (they were hanging down to my bottom teeth). I had to wear a plaster-of-Paris plate across my front teeth through a whole year. I had to drink mostly milkshakes and liquids because I couldn't chew. Thankfully, the teeth eventually grew back.

Rocking my life away: Ever since I can remember, I have rocked back and forth. I wasn't even aware of it. It was a habit, I guess, like marching to a different drum or a beat in my head keeping time to a song I was writing subconsciously - something like that.

Coral Baptist Church was right at the end of my street. That's where I went to church. Woody Watkins was the preacher and we all loved him. At church one Sunday, I saw a guy sitting on the hood of his car in the parking lot surrounded by girls, playing his guitar. His name was "Snuffy" Smith. I knew right then that's what I wanted to do.

Survival of the Fittest: The next year I started high school and formed my first band, made up of high school pals. We were playing a school function when Snuffy came backstage and said, "I gotta join your band." I was thrilled! We spent most of our teenage years together. He was like the brother I never had. Another kid, two years younger than I was, joined the band on lead guitar. He was great. His name was Wayne Gray (he later wrote "Cradle of Love," a Johnny Preston hit). We played around the Miami area for the next couple of years at clubs and for square dances. Some of the club dates were knock-down, drag-outs, but we somehow managed to survive.

"Happy Harold," a country DJ in Miami, had a show and dance every Saturday night called the Old South Jamboree. Snuffy and I played there on occasion, as did some local entertainers. One of these was Donny Lytle who later moved to Nashville, joined Faron Young's band, and changed his name to Donny Young. After moving to Nashville, he recorded a few singles with Decca Records. Then he changed his name again to Johnny Paycheck. Not much later he had a monster hit: "Take this Job and Shove it."

Bill Johnson, a steel guitar player and singer, was also one of the performers on the Jamboree. Bill wrote the hit song "A Wound Time Can't Erase" and recorded it on a local label under Sky Johnson. Stonewall Jackson later recorded it and had the hit on it. Bill later moved to Nashville and played steel for Marty Robbins for a number of years. Carol Norris and Peggy King were sisters and both singers on the show. Charlie McCoy was a featured artist (more about him later).

Jimmy Voytek, a rockabilly singer and one of my best friends, was a regular there. Charlie Justice, a fiddle player who later worked with George Jones and Tammy Wynette, was part of the band. Glen McQuirt (Glen Ray), the steel player who wrote "I Just Came Home to Count the Memories" (recorded by John Anderson) filled in sometimes. Bill Phillips, who became a well-known country singer, was always there as well as Gwen and Jerry Collins, a duet team who later moved to Nashville and recorded for several record companies. Also, there was Slim Somerville, Sr. and many others.

Around this time I met the Rouse Brothers, Ervin and Gordon. Ervin wrote "Orange Blossom Special" and "Sweeter Than the Flowers." Many fiddle players say Ervin Rouse was probably the greatest fiddler that ever held a bow. Ervin used to come into some of the clubs where we were playing and get up and play. He was an alcoholic and lived in a shack in the Everglades. He only came out once in a while. He would get up and play two or three songs and leave. They say he was a little on the crazy side, but I always liked him.

Hank Cutshaw who headed up the Homestead Jamboree in Homestead, Florida, called me one day and said he needed a fiddle player for a Saturday night. He was looking for a guy to just play one square dance two times and did I know someone? It paid ten bucks. I told him I'd find someone. I went down to the pawn shop and bought a five-dollar fiddle that I didn't know how to play. I just figured, "How hard can it be?" Well, I practiced all day on it and got to where I could play the basics to

"Bile Them Cabbage Down," a very simple tune. Then I called Hank back and said, "I can do it." I went down that Saturday night, got up, and played the fiddle badly - twice. I got my ten bucks.

During that time, I auditioned for "Cracker Jim" Brooker, a popular DJ in Miami. He said he wanted to do a TV show centered around me. He was going to call it "Cactus Jim's Talent Ranch Featuring Kent Westberry and Band" complete with our own square dancers and guest artists. The guest artists consisted of girls I went to high school with who could sing. It was a thirty-minute show every Saturday on Channel 17. That gig lasted about a year. I was still in high school.

My mother made all our outfits. They looked like the Grand Ole Opry suits they were wearing at the time. We were still playing clubs at night and going to school in the daytime. Donny Young, who I mentioned before, sat in with us at the club sometimes while we were playing. He also played steel guitar with us a few times.

Chapter 2

WHOLE LOTTA SHAKIN'

*T*hen a new singer started setting the world on fire in the mid-fifties, a guy named Elvis Presley. That guy changed everything! Suddenly none of the clubs wanted country music anymore, so we started playing rockabilly music. Even country music changed a little. Country artists recorded rockabilly under different names. For instance, George Jones recorded under "Thumper Jones," Buck Owens was "Corky Jones," Webb Pierce was "Shady Wall," Leon Payne became "Rock Rogers." There were quite a few others.

We played at a place called The Bird Bowl Lounge for a long time. The owner hated country music, so I devised a plan: we did country anyway, stuff like "Crazy Arms" as well as Buck Owens' songs and Hank Williams' songs. We just put a rock and roll backbeat to them. He loved 'em all!

The first time I met Charlie McCoy was at the house of a friend, Jim Isbell. He played drums with Charlie, and we went to hear Charlie play. He had about a six-piece band and played more blues than we did. Still, we became fast friends. We had the top two bands in the area and even worked together some. I guess Charlie could play any instrument there was, even what they call a "recorder" - I believe that's what they call the flute-like instrument they play to charm snakes out of baskets in India. More about Charlie later.

In 1959 I decided I wanted a J-200 Gibson guitar, but one unlike any guitar anyone else had. I drew one up on a piece of paper, took it to a local music store, and asked if I could have Gibson make it for me. They did. The guitar was the first and only guitar Gibson ever made with all six tuning knobs on one side and an "elf shoe" head. There wasn't enough room to put the Gibson name on the neck, so they just put a "G." The guitar was almost snow white with two black, custom-made guard plates with my name on one of them. It was beautiful! That guitar cost me $750, and it took me two years to pay it off.

The Phillip Morris Country Music Show came to town starring Carl Smith, Goldie Hill, Red Sovine, Mimi Roman, Ronnie Self, Mel Tillis, George Morgan, and Little Jimmy Dickens. Cracker Jim asked us to open the show, which we did. Backstage, I met Mel Tillis. He said, "I saw your TV show, and you were good. You should be in Nashville. If you get up there, look me up." I thought that was awfully nice of him but told myself, "Everyone says that."

Cracker Jim used to bring Opry acts down from Nashville to the Dade County Auditorium. He'd let Snuffy and me backstage to meet them all. The Wilburn Brothers, Doyle and Teddy, were very nice; I remember Doyle saying, "If you are thinking about getting into the music business, don't! Do something else." It didn't change my mind. Cracker Jim then took me to Nashville in 1959 for the DJ Convention, and he got me on the Ernest Tubb Record Shop Show. I borrowed George Hamilton IV's guitar. I love Nashville. I thought, "Here's where I want to be!" We spent about three days there before going back home to Miami.

I thought it was time to record something. Art Records was in North Miami. They and a few other local labels had some pretty good rockabilly singers on their labels - Tommy Spurlin, Mike Shaw, Leon Douglas, Wes Hardin, and Jimmy Tennant (who later changed his name to Jimmy Velvet, then Velbit), to name a few. I had written a rockabilly song called "My Baby Don't Rock Me Now." Wayne Gray, Snuffy and me along with a drummer, Lou Stewart, went to Art Records and played the song for Hal Doane, the owner. He liked what he heard and asked if we had something to put on the other side. I said, "Yes, I just wrote one called 'No Place to Park.'" I had renamed my band "The Chaperones." We cut it. The record came out in 1958. It didn't set the world on fire - but it *did* get listed in the Rockabilly Hall of Fame.

For about three weeks I took a gig as a single, playing the intermission of the "Bullmoose" Jackson Show at the old Rockin' MB Lounge, later known as the Peppermint Lounge, on Miami Beach. It was a very famous club in the 1950s. It was known as the Troubador. Bullmoose was a nice man and king of the sax. He was well known in the jazz and rhythm and blues circles.

Sticky Business: I had quit school by then, in the eleventh grade, to focus more on music. I was playing clubs till three a.m. and getting up at seven a.m. to get ready for school - something had to go! Then Wayne Gray met a guy who wanted to do a string of dates throughout Florida. His name was Buck Trail. Buck had a couple of records out himself called "Knocked Out Joint On Mars" and "Honky Tonk on 2nd Street" on Trail Records. We joined up with him. We worked a lot of shows in Florida and played drive-in movies on top of the concession stands and local movie theaters. He wanted to have something to sell at the shows, so he made a deal with Art Records to buy a few hundred of my records, then change the label to Trail Records. We sat up for days gluing Trail labels over Art labels.

We were playing a five-and-ten-cent store in Sebring, Florida, when I met up with a girl I had gone to high school with. Her name was Grace. We started dating, and she would follow us around the different places we were playing. I'll explain more about her later.

The Art Records people called. They had a woman who had written some songs and wanted someone with a band to do a session with them. He said she'd pay us. We went back to Miami and recorded

"Popcorn and Candy Bars" and "Turkish Doghouse Rock." It didn't do much either! That's when Snuffy went to Nashville to check things out, and I formed a new band. We worked sock hops and Bob Green shows. Bob was a local DJ and pretty well known in the 1950s. He was the local version of Dick Clark at the time. He later married Anita Bryant.

I got a new booking agent who had us booked in a club in Atlanta, Georgia. Grace and I were still dating. She drove up with us, and we decided to get married. One afternoon we went to Jonesboro, Georgia, a few miles from Atlanta, and we were married. My parents and her mom weren't too happy about it.

The club we were working in was a nice place. William Talman (the DA on *The Perry Mason Show*) came in every night to see us. Also, Doug Kershaw of the Rusty and Doug team would come in and get up and sing. Doug was in the army and stationed there. I knew all the Rusty and Doug songs, so I sang tenor with Doug. After the gig ended, we headed back to Miami.

I worked Cathy's Carnival Club a couple of miles down the road from where Jack Blanchard used to play with Donel Austin before he met Misty Morgan and married her. I had played the Coral Lounge in Hollywood, Florida, and Misty would play and sing pop tunes on piano during our intermissions. Jack and Misty were friends of mine. Later they had the big hit "Tennessee Bird Walk" and many other successful songs.

When the contract ended at Cathy's, I told the band I was going to Nashville. Wayne Gray and Snuffy, who had just come back from Music City, said they'd go with me. I told Grace, "Wait here. I'll go up, get a job, look around for a place to stay, and then send for you."

My first band in high school – left to right – Ray Knowles, Snuffy Smith, Wayne Gray, and Kent.

Kent and custom Gibson guitar.

Jerry Johnson, drums. Don McGinnis, bass.
Kent CW Keith guitar – (chaperones).

The chaperones – Kent in middle, Snuffy Smith (bass), Wayne Gray (guitar).

Kent on Ernest Tubb Record Shop. Midnite Jamboree. 1960.

Standing – left to right – Ray Knowles, Jim Yelvington, Ritchie Register – Kneeling: Franklin Morrell, Kent, Snuffy Smith.

Chapter 3

MUSIC CITY, HERE WE COME!

*W*e arrived in Nashville. A feeling hit me like nothing I had ever felt before. It was like a magical place. I can't describe that feeling. Nashville had become a place you'd never want to leave!

We didn't have much money, so we checked into the YMCA on Seventh Avenue. We paid seven dollars a week. Right across the street was the old Clarkston Hotel where a lot of country artists would congregate in the restaurant in the afternoon. Marty Robbins, Faron Young, The Wilburn Brothers, and lots of others would hang out there. The WSM Building was down the same street a few blocks away. That's where they held the Friday Night Frolics. I remember Snuffy and I sat on the porch of the YMCA and wrote a song called "She Won't Let Me Forget Her (She's Afraid That I Will)" which was later recorded by Bob Wills and the Texas Playboys for KAPP Records.

Back then most of the publishers were on Seventh Avenue. They were all in the same building across the hall from each other. I went to Tree Music the next day and met Buddy Killen and Bill Anderson, another great writer. I played some songs for Buddy. He wasn't too impressed, but he took two of my songs: "Changed My Mind" recorded by Billy Walker and "Loveland" cut by Billy Grammar. Neither one made any money to speak of. Right about then I felt like things were going a bit too slow.

I was walking in downtown Nashville early one evening. In a Harvey's Department Store window, I saw a girl mannequin all dressed up. I thought to myself, "Man! I wish you could talk." I guess I was feeling a little lonesome. I went back to the YMCA and wrote "The Model Made of Clay" with Wayne Gray about an old man who loves a department store mannequin and visits her at night. Roughly, the idea went like this: every night at ten o'clock, the storekeeper locks his shop containing pretty gowns and the latest fashions on display. There's an old, gray-haired man standing outside in the cold, looking in the window at a model made of clay and so forth. Roger Miller heard the song later at a friend's house and wanted to record it, but his producer, Buddy Killen, wouldn't let him. Roger hadn't hit yet, so he couldn't pick and choose what he wanted to record. The song never got recorded.

We got a job here and there, just enough to enable us to move to a rundown motel room. After a while Grace came up. Her mother had given her some money. Grace and I were able to scrape up enough to rent a house. On top of it all, Grace was pregnant, and we weren't getting along very well. A few months later we had a beautiful daughter. I came up with the name DeBeaux, pronounced "Debo." It's French. We finally split up, and Grace went back home to Miami.

I remember later walking down a sidewalk in downtown Nashville when I turned the corner and ran right into Mel Tillis. He stopped me and said, "You're that g..g..guy from mi...mi...Miami, uh, Fu..Fu...Florida, that I met at the Phillip Morris show!"

I said, "Yes, I am."

He said, "Who are y...y...y..you writing for?" I told him that I wasn't writing for anyone yet. He said, "Come along with mu..mu...me." Right then he took me to meet Jim Denny, owner of Cedarwood Publishing Company! I went into the office, and Mel said, "Jim, you need to sign this boy as a writer and singer." Jim signed me - as a writer.

A few days later Wayne Gray and I were sitting in the office. We had just written a song when Mel came in and said, "I'll cut that!" The song was "That's Where the Hurt Comes In." It became the flip side of "Hearts of Stone" on Columbia. Jim Denny asked Snuffy and me if we wanted to cut a record ourselves. We said sure. The next day we had a meeting with Don Law with Columbia Records and Jim Vinneau with MGM. Jim said we could choose which one we wanted! We chose MGM - because Hank Williams, one of my heroes, recorded for MGM.

We went into the studio with two songs - one I had just written called "Bye, Bye, Buddy." For the flip side, we did a Marijohn Wilkin song, "Billy Blue Eyes." Floyd Cramer played a *celeste* - an unusual instrument for country music - on the "Blue Eyes" side. I asked Wayne Moss to play lead guitar because I loved his style of playing. Wayne played in Charlie McCoy's band. Hank Garland and Grady Martin had been scheduled to play the session and were none too happy about being replaced. They left the session. Later Wayne and Charlie McCoy formed the "Area Code 615" band, and Wayne formed the rock group "Barefoot Jerry." Wayne was married to a girl named Jerri, and she used to go around barefoot a lot. Any connection? Probably not!

At that time, Nashville had pinball machines and blackjack tables that paid off in most of the bars. The bars even had a little peephole in the entrance door, like in the old speakeasy days. The cops still knew what was going on. When they would come by and ring the doorbell, the dealer would break down the blackjack tables in a heartbeat and shove them behind something. The cop would come in, check the place out, then leave. In a flash, the operation would be back up and running. The Wagon Wheel Club next door to Tootsie's Orchid Lounge was one of those places. It was a small place. The Sleepy LaBeef Trio and Casanova Jack often played there.

Tootsie's was painted purple on the outside. *Everyone* went to Tootsie's. To some, it was just a beer joint, to others it was "home."

Tootsie was like a mother to everyone. If you were broke, she'd come up and slip a twenty-dollar bill in your pocket. She'd say, "Pay me back when you get it." She was famous for the long hatpin she carried around. If you got loud and unruly, she'd give you a hard jab with it – and did it hurt! I must admit I was her pincushion a few times.

One night I was sitting in the Wagon Wheel with Roger Miller when a new writer in town came in and joined us. Roger introduced him as Willie Nelson.

Roger took me under his wing and introduced me to everyone he could. He helped me a lot. Willie, Harlan Howard, and Hank Co-chran all came to Nashville about the same time. Even though Roger wrote for Tree Music and I wrote for Cedarwood, we thought nothing of helping each other. All the writers I knew did the same.

Chapter 4

FUN AND GAMES

Nashville was a party town. There were parties going on every night at someone's house. Beer, pills, and girls flowed like a river. A lot of writers and artists would get together and play their latest songs. At any given party you might see Justin Tubb, Faron Young, Little Jimmy Dickens, Carl Belew, Georgie Riddle, Willie Nelson, Roger Miller, Ira Louvin, Darrell McCall, Earl Scott - and me. A lot of songs got written and recorded that way. During the Grand Ole Opry on Saturday night, many artists would walk across the alley separating Tootsie's from the Ryman Auditorium during their breaks and have a beer or visit. Those were some fun times.

Linebaugh's Restaurant was right across the street from Tootsie's. After Tootsie's closed at midnight, everyone would congregate there. A lot of the writers and musicians down on their luck would order a cup of hot water, then mix in a little ketchup and a pack of crackers to make Poor Boy's Tomato Soup. Didn't taste too bad, either.

Trials of a Truck Drivin' Man: I had to have some cash coming in, so I went out and got a job driving a tractor-trailer loaded with milk to go to Murfreesboro to supply milk delivery trucks. The regular truck driver rode with me the first two days to show me how to drive the rig. It was an old Diamond T with a double clutch gear-shift. On the third day he didn't show up. I waited thirty minutes for him, then figured he wanted me to go on by myself. I hopped into the truck, started her up, and took off. The only thing was, I hadn't memorized the roads I was supposed to take to get there. Back then there were no interstates, so from East Nashville to Donelson you had to take the ferry boat at the landing.

Trouble was, you couldn't take a tractor-trailer rig on the ferry. I had come down a steep hill to get there. I knew I couldn't back that big ol' trailer up that hill, so I put the air brakes on and turned the wheel as far as I could to the curb. There was a steep, three-foot ditch on the right. I turned off the engine and walked up to a house to ask to use the phone to call the company. The people who lived there were nice enough to get up at six a.m. to let me use their phone. I called the office, and they weren't too happy to hear from me. They said they'd send the driver right out. When he got there, he was a little upset, you might say, and before I could tell him anything, he jumped in the truck, started it up, and threw it in gear. Whoops! The truck ran smack off the road into the ditch! They had to unload all that milk and call for another truck. Needless to say, I got fired. That ended my brief career as a truck driver.

I tried several other jobs, but none panned out. One was selling graveyard plots. The only trouble was no one was thinking about dying. I worked a whole week without selling one. I did a lot of walking. I even got to thinking about a tree removal service using a hungry woodpecker or two but I couldn't find one. What to do? I decided to go write another song.

Thankfully, financial relief was just around the corner. I landed my first road gig. It was with Cousin Jody (Tex Summey) playing rhythm guitar and singing a couple of songs. It was in Illinois, I think, with Miss Jerry Johnson on bass. It went well. When we got back to Nashville Jody said, "The boy rocked all the way from Nashville to Illinois and never shut his eyes."

I got called to do a show in South Carolina with Jimmy C. Newman. I loved working with Jimmy. He would go into a restaurant and order a couple of *hen fruits* (eggs) and a glass of *moo juice* (milk). He had that Cajun lingo down pat.

One evening I was sitting on the couch and thinking of my daughter, DeBeaux. She was about one or two by now. I picked up my guitar and wrote "Air Mail to Heaven," about a little girl who writes a letter to her daddy in heaven. The mailman reads it to find he's the new man taking her daddy's place with her mom.

Chapter 5

SESSIONS AND SUCH

B reaking the Ice: I remember one day Jim Denny told me to come to all his demo sessions and hang out at the studio. Then when they got a slot open, I could put one of my songs down. Mel Tillis, Marijohn Wilkin and Wayne Walker were Cedarwood's main writers. After the first two sessions I still hadn't got to put one song down. I was beginning to think, "This ain't working." Then on the third one, with 30 minutes to go in the session, Mel, Marijohn and Wayne all got into a fight with Jim Denny. I don't know what it was about, but they all walked out. Denny said, "Kent, do you have something to put down?" Well, it was about time! I put down "Air Mail to Heaven." Carl Smith later had a top ten record with it. Denny was very impressed. I also put down "Of All the Things You Left, It's Me That Hurts the Most," later recorded by Little Jimmy Dickens and Jimmy Newman, and finally, "If Heartaches Were Wine, I'd Stay Drunk All the Time," cut by Stonewall Jackson. I was in – FINALLY!!!

Jim Denny said, "Kent, I want to pair you up with Marijohn Wilkin and let you hone your writing skills with her." I was on board. We would write two or three times each week. One of those meetings produced "I Just Don't Understand," which I had written as an instrumental.

Marijohn said, "Let's put some lyrics to that." I agreed. In about twenty minutes it was done.

Around this time, a guy named Johnny Ferguson had a hit on a song called "Angela Jones." He was putting a band together to go to Toronto, Canada, to work the Edison Hotel. He hired Snuffy and me to go, but we needed a lead guitar player. We called Charlie McCoy. Charlie was still in Miami and wanting to come to Nashville. Charlie came right up, but by the time he arrived, Johnny had hired a guitar player. We still needed a drummer, so Charlie became our drummer.

When we got back to Nashville we needed a place to stay again. We ran into three girls from Michigan who had rented an older house on Music Row and were getting ready to go back home. They had six more days left on their rent. They said if we slept in the attic until they left, we could move in and stay till their rent was up. We did.

The first night we were all sleeping when, about three a.m., I woke up with a big rat sitting on my chest! Next morning the girls were gone. The girls had left behind half a bag of stale potato chips. We had breakfast! Snuffy had one quarter left, so we went downtown to Linebaugh's. Snuffy put the quarter in the pinball machine and hit it for twenty dollars. We bought groceries!

It wasn't long after that Charlie and I got together with Bill "Groover" Aiken, piano player with Charlie's band, "The Escorts," Jim Isbell, drummer from Miami who later worked with Jerry Lee Lewis for a number of years, and Tony Moon, lead guitar player and producer, who had worked with Buzz Cason and The Casuals. We all moved into a beautiful, five-bedroom home in Madison. A pilot for one of the airlines owned it. He said he wasn't going to use it and we could rent it from him. We all would have our own space. We kicked in about fifty bucks per month each. It was a good deal for everyone. We had a party pad!

Guess I'll Take a Shower: Little Jimmy Dickens lived right down the street and sometimes he would come over. Roger Miller would drop by, and Charlie's whole band would come over and rehearse.

Girls would come over to hang around. One morning I woke up and found a girl asleep in the bathtub.

Charlie found a big, roomy place in East Nashville upstairs over a motorcycle shop. He rented it and started "The Sack Club" - no alcoholic beverages, just hot dogs, chips, and cokes. It was a place where high school kids could go and dance. Charlie and the band played on weekends. Different guest artists would drop in and play. Snuffy and I played there a couple of times. It was a popular hangout for about a year or so.

Ann-Margret came to town and heard "I Just Don't Understand." Charlie had played harmonica on it. Ann recorded it, and it turned out to be a hit! One afternoon I was in Chet Atkins' office, and Chet introduced me to Ann. She came running over, kissed me on the cheek, and said, "Thanks for the song!" I thanked her for singing it. Later, Les Paul and Mary Ford had a single on it as well. That song enabled me to get a draw of seventy-five dollars a week against my royalties, which made things a little easier. In 1994 The Beatles released the song on a CD, *Live at the BBC*. More about that later.

At some point in time, Archie Bleyer (Arthur Godfrey's former musical director) at Cadence Records took a liking to Charlie McCoy and wanted to do a record on him. Charlie came to me and said, "I got this song from a friend of mine called 'Cherry Berry Wine.' It's only partially written. You want to help me with it?" I said sure, and we wrote it. The song was Charlie's first vocal record, reaching Billboard's Pop Chart at number ninety-nine.

Bill (Groover) Aiken and I became close friends. He knew Audrey Williams, Hank's wife. She still lived in the original house that she and Hank shared. It was a ranch-type brick home with a party room over the garage. Audrey had lots of parties back then, and I was invited to a few of them. She even showed me the inside of the house. On the wall in the master bedroom was a portrait of Hank, about seven-foot by six-foot, in a wood-and-gold frame. Surrounding the house was a wrought iron fence with the music notes to "Lovesick Blues" on it. Bill and I went swimming in her pool quite a bit. It was there I met Sue Everly, ex-wife of Don Everly of the Everly Brothers, and we became friends.

Later on, in the late 1980s, Tammy Wynette and husband, George Ritchie, bought the Hank Williams home. They dismantled it piece by piece, brick by brick, and someone rebuilt it down on Music Row as a tourist attraction. But no one came to see it. Then they made a bar out of it. Almost nobody went. It wasn't there too long until it disappeared. In my opinion, someone ruined a country music treasure.

Chapter 6

HIT THE ROAD, JACK

You Can Take the Boy Out of the Country, But…: It was during this time I got a call from Jim Denny asking me if I wanted to go on tour with Carl Perkins. "Holy Wallflowers!" Of course I did! He wanted Snuffy too. I worked with Carl for about a year and loved every minute of it. Carl was one of the nicest guys I ever worked with. I recall the time we were pulling a little teardrop trailer and riding along in "Ole Blue" – that's what he called the Buick we traveled in - and we were heading for Las Vegas. It was about three in the morning, and I was trying to sleep in the back seat when suddenly I heard the loudest commotion coming from the trunk! I said, "Carl, what in the heck is that racket in the back?" He smiled, pulled over to the side of the road, and motioned for me to get out. I went around to the back of the car while Carl opened the trunk. There were cages of crickets! He grinned and said, "Old Carl just wanted to take a little country to the city."

There were five of us in the car - Carl, his younger brother Clayton, Snuffy, a drummer, and me. Clayton had a mean streak in him and at times would pick a fight with anyone. One time we were on top of Pike's Peak and Carl slammed on the brakes, went around, and snatched Clayton out of the car. They went at it. Carl won, of course! They got back in the car and we rode on.

Carl said that one time he was a guest on the Red Foley Show, the Ozark Jubilee, about the time Carl's "Blue Suede Shoes" reached the top. They were setting up for the show, and Red told Carl and the band where he wanted them to be. Clayton didn't like it, so he hauled off and hit Mr. Foley, knocking him down. Sometimes they would be working a club in Memphis and a fight would break out. Clayton would jump off the stage into the pile and join right in.

Spray That Again: We worked with Carl on several trips to Vegas. On another trip, we took Bill (Groover) Aiken on piano and a drummer by the name of Dewey Martin, who later found fame in the Buffalo Springfield rock group. We were working the Golden Nugget in Vegas. One night, just before going on, I heard Carl holler, "Oh my gosh!"

I said, "What's wrong, Carl?" He showed me. He had grabbed the wrong can of spray and sprayed blue suede shoe dressing all over his hair. No one else seemed to notice.

One night after our show, a man approached Snuffy and I and said he'd like to schedule a screen test for us in Hollywood for a movie called *Teenage Millionaire* starring Jimmy Clanton (who had the hit record *Just a Dream* in the 1950s). He wanted to fly us out the next morning. It would've meant leaving Carl without two band members in the middle of a gig. I couldn't do it. I told him no.

We worked the Nugget with Carl quite a bit over the next year. We worked opposite such stars as Bob Wills and his Texas Playboys, Judy Lynn, The Sneed Family, Hank Thompson and The Brazos Valley Boys, Jimmy Wakely, and Wanda Jackson - all at different times, of course. Wanda had just recorded "Right or Wrong," and it was a hit. I had the B-side "Funnel of Love" which did nothing at the time. More about that later.

Carl said Wynn Stewart was playing the Nashville Nevada Club in Las Vegas and asked if we wanted to go see him. Wynn was one of my very favorite singers, so we went. Wynn took us upstairs to his office, and we all had some drinks and passed the guitar around. What a great evening!

We met The Newton Brothers, Wayne and his brother Jerry, who were working across the street from the Golden Nugget. That was before Wayne Newton became a household name. We used to go catch their show sometimes when we were off. They were just kids at the time. We met a lot of good people in Vegas. You never knew when to go to bed - you were afraid you might miss something.

Many nights after work, Carl would send me across the street to the liquor store for a bottle of "Early Times" bourbon. He and I would sit on the floor in his room and talk for hours and play songs. He talked about the Lord a lot. He was a good Christian man. He drank a lot back then, but I never saw him drunk. Later on, when he joined Johnny Cash, he quit drinking altogether. He joined Johnny after Luther Perkins died. By the way, Luther was no relation to Carl.

On a couple of occasions Carl invited The Hank Thompson Band and other entertainers at the Nugget over to the motel, and he would fry chicken and make mashed potatoes for all of them. Carl would sit on the floor with a guitar and sing Hank Williams' songs with big ole tears running down his face. Everyone else had goosebumps all over their arms. Carl was a soul man.

Chapter 7

RUBBIN' ELBOWS AND WRITIN' SONGS

*E*very October came the DJ Convention, a place where DJs could meet the artists and songwriters. It was like party week. All the hotels downtown catered to the DJs. I met Slim Whitman, Buck Owens, Johnny Horton, and Charlie Rich there, along with Bobby Helms, who had "Fraulein" and "My Special Angel." Later Bobby recorded two of my songs, "Guess We Thought the World Would End" and "Mary Goes 'Round." You could meet everybody that was anybody in country music at the DJ Convention. It was a magical time.

I had known Darrell McCall and Charlie Dick, Patsy Cline's husband, and Georgie Riddle pretty well. We used to hang out at Tootsie's. Tootsie had a game of electronic shuffleboard. I would play her for beers. If I won, she'd mark an ink line on her wall. I had a lot of lines there and drank free a lot. I think some of those beer lines are still on her wall.

That's where I met Carl Belew the first time. Carl was a great songwriter. He wrote "Lonely Street," "Stop the World and Let Me Off," "Am I that Easy to Forget?" and "What's He Doing in My World?" along with lots of other good ones. He was from Salina, Kansas. He would come into town every so often and pitch his songs. If he ran short of money, he would sell half a song for enough money to party a little longer. He sold part of "Lonely Street" and a few more. Carl recorded one of my songs - his first hit! "Hello Out There" won me my first BMI award!

Back then almost everyone in the music business took pills to stay awake and had pill parties. Carl Belew was a practical joker. I remember everyone was having a party one time. They'd been up for about two days, still picking and singing, having a great time. Carl came in and set a bag of pills on the table. He said, "Enjoy," and left. A little while later everyone was sound asleep. He had brought sleeping pills to the party! He laughed about that for weeks.

I met Eddie White, who later recorded under the name of Johnny Darrell, at one of the parties along with Bobby Goldsboro, Waylon Jennings, and others. We were all passing the guitar around, playing our latest songs. Bobby played "Honey," and Johnny wanted to record it. Johnny was the first to record "Green, Green Grass of Home," "Mental Revenge," and "Ruby, Don't Take Your Love to Town." He got covered every time by someone else, and they had the hits on them!

Whenever we ran short of money, Wayne Gray, Snuffy Smith, and I would go back to Miami and work the Bird Bowl Lounge for a few months till we made enough to go back to Nashville. Wayne was married about this time and so was Snuffy. I was divorced. I was still living with Charlie and the guys at the party pad in Madison.

I went down to Cedarwood one afternoon and Mel was there. I said, "Mel, I got a great idea for a song."

He said, "What is it?"

I said, "'Sorrow's Tearing Down the House (That Happiness once Built)'."

Mel said, "Get your guitar." We went into the office, and about fifteen minutes later, we had it. Porter Wagoner and Skeeter Davis recorded it first. Later Porter recorded it with Dolly Parton. Then Little Jimmy Dickens and Stonewall Jackson recorded it. Right after that Gene McDaniels who had "A Hundred Pounds of Clay" recorded one of my and Marijohn's songs, "She's Come Back." It reached number forty-nine in the Billboard pop charts. About this time, I found out the rock group Freddie and The Dreamers had recorded "I Just Don't Understand," and it was in their *Best Of* Capital album.

Carl and Pearl Butler recorded a song I wrote for a girl who was just a friend and never dated because she was too much like me. I don't know if that's good or bad. The song was "We'd Destroy Each other." We got word that Sammy Davis Jr. had recorded a song of mine and Wayne Gray's titled "The Fool I Used to Be" for a single. A few months later Carl Perkins did it too.

Chapter 8

YOU'RE IN THE ARMY NOW!

*I*n 1962 I received word that my favorite uncle, Sam, wanted me - a draft notice! "Kiss Aunt Agnes and hug Aunt Suzie." It was a request I couldn't ignore. Three mornings later an army bus pulled up in our driveway. Just like that, I was Private James Kent Westberry. I never used my first name. It was always Kent. I guess that's because I thought if someone walked into a crowded room and hollered, "James!" about thirty-five people would yell, "WHAT?"

I was dumbfounded, but I loved my country and my God. I said to myself, "I'll do the best I can." And I did! One thing's for certain: I went in as a kid and came out a man. The army will mature you in a hurry; it'll grow you up fast!

Rock on, Soldier: I went through the inoculation process. The army doctor asked me if I had any physical defects. Looked maybe like a chance to be rejected! Quickly I said, "Yes, sir. I rock back and forth a lot." The doc scribbled on the paper, "He rocks," then turned and hollered, "NEXT!"

Don't Count Me Out Quite Yet: Going through basic training in Fort Chaffee, Arkansas, I had one small setback. After a seven-mile march in blazing hot sun then drinking a canteen of cold water, I caught pneumonia. I went on sick call with a fever of 104. They put me in the hospital. I don't remember a thing about it till I woke up ten days later and there was a priest reading last rites over me. I said, "What's going on?" What a weird feeling - I guess they figured I wasn't going to survive. I did. Then I had to take the whole eight weeks of basic training all over again. Finally, I made it through!

One day we were on the infiltration course. That's where you crawl on your belly through barbed wire while *real* machine gun rounds are zooming just over your head. The man next to me yelled my name and said he didn't feel good. He said he felt real dizzy. I hollered, "STOP!" All firing ceased. It turned out the automatic machine gun had fired a rare "light round" which had struck the guy in the throat. We never found out what happened to him. They closed Fort Chaffee down. There were generals and top brass all over the place.

My second eight weeks was in Fort Sill, Oklahoma. One night I heard that Little Jimmy Dickens was going to be at the Southern Club in town. Jimmy had recorded one of my songs, "It's Me That Hurts the Most." I asked my sergeant if I could go see him. He said okay and gave me a pass. When I got to the hotel where Jimmy was checked in, I called from the lobby. He answered the phone. When he heard it was me, he invited me up to his room. I went into the room and Jim was shaving. I told him I was stationed there, then said I got a great song idea: "Little Jack Daniels" (I had met him at a bar one time). We wrote the song right there in about twenty minutes.

In Jimmy's closet I had noticed boxes of .45 records he was going to sell at the show that night. Stamped on each box was "Handle with Care." I said what about this for a ballad, "Handle with Care (Please Treat Her Gently, I Broke Her Heart A Long Time Ago)." We wrote that one, too, then went on to the show. Afterwards, I went back to base. Jimmy recorded both songs before I got out of the service.

The Vietnam thing was just starting to kick up. They were sending some troops over there and some to Germany. I was sent to Hanau, Germany, in a 155mm howitzer division. On the way over on the boat, I was sitting cross-legged on the deck rocking back and forth. The guys offered to pay me well if I'd just stop rocking. They were all seasick. I was comfortable as could be.

Over there in my off time, I played a little music with "The Hometowners," a group that Pat Patterson had been in when he was there. Pat had just rotated back home and I kinda filled his spot. That was in 1962.

Sad News from Home: I was walking guard duty at the ammo dump, the place where they store the ammunition, when I got word that President John F. Kennedy had been shot. We were on full alert for the next few weeks. After that, not much really happened out of the ordinary during the next two years. One afternoon I was reading the *Stars and Stripes* newspaper in barracks when I saw a headline: "Jim Denny with Cedarwood Publishing Company Dies." A good-sized piece of my world died right then.

Sorry, I Have a Previous Engagement: One day at mail call I got a letter from Nashville saying I was invited to the awards dinner to accept a BMI award for "Hello Out There." I was in a homemade igloo in thirty-five below zero and snow up to my butt. What a bummer! At least I kept writing songs in the barracks in my spare time.

Chapter 9

WORKING WITH AMERICA'S
BELOVED COWBOY

I got out of the service honorably in February of 1964. I took a train from Fort Dix, New Jersey, to Nashville. Wayne Gray picked me up at Union Station and took me straight to the party pad. I couldn't wait to see Charlie and the gang again. When I got there only Groover was there. He said Charlie had gotten married and moved out. All the others had gone, and he, too, was fixing to move. Another bummer. I moved in with Wayne Gray and his wife for the time being.

Bill Denny, Jim's oldest son, had taken over as head of Cedarwood. Bill was more business-oriented than anything else. His interests were more in line with banking, properties, and such than the music business. Within a year Mel Tillis, Marijohn Wilkin, and Wayne Walker had all quit and started their own publishing companies. Jim's youngest son, John, started his own company later. My contract wasn't up yet, so I stayed on.

One night I was downtown and ran into Dale Ward in one of the clubs. Dale had the hit record, *A Letter to Sherry*. He was set to record the next day. I told him I had a song for him. We went to his place, and I played the song for him. It was "A Woman Made Man." He recorded it on Boyd Records.

Meanwhile, Wayne Gray had been working with Tex Ritter. Wayne called and asked if I wanted a job playing with Tex. Jumpin' Jehosephat! Of course I did! On the first tour I made with Tex, he asked Wayne, "Does the boy rock when he drives?"

Wayne replied, "As a matter of fact, he does."

Tex frowned and said, "Good God, it looks like I'm gonna do a lot of drivin'." Tex got used to it eventually.

Tex had us all join the Country Music Association - he eventually became president. I have to say, I loved Tex. I think everyone that ever met him did. He called everyone he met "John." I asked him once, "Why do you call everyone John?"

He said, "About 80% of the time I'll be right." At the time, Tex's band consisted of just me and Wayne, Wayne on lead and me on rhythm guitar. Wayne and I did all the driving. Every now and then Tex would want to drive. He was good for about two miles, then he'd start dozing off. One of us would take over.

On one of our trips, we picked Tex up in California. He said we were invited to Johnny Cash's house for dinner. We went. Johnny lived on the side of a mountain in Burbank. His house was a sprawling, ranch-type home. I remember Johnny's pool room had an indestructible floor, gold in color and full of glitter. I have never seen another one. At that time Johnny was married to his first wife, Vivian.

Back on the road, we talked Tex into hiring a drummer. Billy Sprout (Cosby) joined us. That rounded out "The Bo Weevils," Tex's band. Billy Cosby had a duet team in the late 1950s with Bobby Johnson as The Sprouts. They had several rockabilly records with RCA Vic and Spangler Records. Among their best known was "Teen Billy Baby" and "Goodbye, She's Gone."

Mismatched Feet: Sometimes Tex would come out on stage wearing two different colored boots - left-footed ones at that! We would crack up.

Arkie the Fixer: Speaking of Tex, we were with him on a package show one time when Wayne's back went out. We pulled up at the auditorium backstage a little early. Arkie the Arkansas Woodchopper, the singer-comedian, was there. Tex asked if there was a chiropractor in town. Arkie said, "I'm a chiropractor. What's the problem?"

Tex told him Wayne's back was out. Just like that Arkie popped Wayne's back and fixed him up. Then Arkie looked at Tex and said, "You've got hemorrhoids!"

Tex stared at Arkie and said, "How do you know that?"

Arkie replied, "I can tell by looking at your feet."

Tex puckered his mouth and said, "You mean you can tell I've got hemorrhoids just by looking at my feet?" Arkie nodded yes. Tex said, "Then how about looking up my ass and telling me if I've got my boots on the right feet!"

Back in Nashville, Darrell McCall and I were palling around again. He suggested we share a place. That sounded good to me. Bill Denny had some duplexes for rent on West End, and I got one. Darrell and I moved in.

Darrell was working with Faron Young and I was working with Tex. We had a party one night. Wayne Walker was there, along with Mel Tillis, Benny Joy (a new writer with Cedarwood) and Hugh X. Lewis. I don't remember who else was there. Mel got a guitar, came over to me, and played a song he had started. He said, "Help me finish this." It was "Memory Maker." We had it finished in no time. Mel recorded it later and it reached number three in the Billboard charts. This was my second BMI award winner.

A few weeks later Mel came into Cedarwood and said to me, "I got this song started. What do you think?" He played two lines of it. "I don't care what you do from now on, I'm gonna leave you all alone, I'm gonna be gone" (this became the title). Jimmy Dean recorded it.

We had nicknames at Cedarwood. Mel was "Flutterlips," Wayne Walker was "Fluffo" and, of course, I was "The Rocker." Ronnie Self was a new writer at Cedarwood. He had recorded for Columbia and other labels as a rockabilly singer. Earlier he had written "Sweet No-thin's" and "I'm Sorry," both recorded by Brenda Lee. Ronnie was the nervous type. One day he was unhappy with his BMI royalty state-ments, so he invited everyone on Music Row to attend an award-burning party. He set fire to all his BMI awards on the sidewalk in front of BMI. Although he was way out in left field at times, Ronnie was a great writer. I liked him. We wrote several songs together. His nickname was "Frantic," and he lived up to it. Many years later I heard Ronnie had jumped - or was pushed - off a motel balcony from the fifth floor and died in Missouri, his home state.

Name Droppers: I heard a great story. Stonewall Jackson, Red So-vine, and Del Reeves were riding in Del's car to a show and were stopped by flashing blue lights. The cop came up and asked Del, "What's your name?"

Del said "*Franklin* Delano Reeves," which was his real name. The cop asked Red Sovine the same question. Red said "*Woodrow Wilson* Sovine," his real name. Then the cop glared at Stonewall and in a hard tone, said, "And I suppose you're George Washington?" Stone-wall replied "No, *Stonewall* Jackson." The cop yanked him out of the car and beat him up. I mean, he put Stonewall in the hospital! Later Stonewall sued the city and won.

Benny Joy was a rockabilly artist and a good writer. Benny and I wrote about seventeen songs together, and I think sixteen were recorded. One of them was "The Star of the Show (Won't Be On To-night)." Carl Perkins did that one, as did Red Sovine. Mel recorded another one, "Helpless Hopeless Fool," and Carl Smith cut "Why Do I keep Doing This to Us?" Benny and I were sitting in Cedarwood one afternoon and wondering what we could get into. We heard that James Brown, the godfather of soul, R&B singer, was going to be at the baseball stadium that next afternoon. We decided to go see him. We got to the stadium early. James Brown's bus was parked behind the huge stage complex. I went over and knocked on the door. James opened the door. He didn't have his shirt on. He said, "Hey guys, come on in here!" Benny and I got on the bus. Uh, oh! All his dancing girls were sitting there along with Solomon Burke, who had a big hit on "Just Out of Reach (Of my Two Open Arms)." Others came from the back of the bus and shook our hands. They invited us to stay for the show. We did.

The show was great. Afterward, James and Solomon took us to some of the Black clubs over on Charlotte Avenue, off West End. Benny and I were the only two white guys in these places. They took good care of us and really treated us special. They were such nice guys.

About four months into playing with Tex, we were working a big show with Buck Owens, Jan Howard, Faron Young (Darrell was on the show), and several other acts. Ten minutes before show time Tex said, "Tonight you'll start playing bass for me." *Me!?* I said, "Tex, I don't know your songs on bass."

He smiled and said, "Now's a good time to learn." The show started. I kept searching all over that bass neck trying to find where he was at! At long last the show ended and we went back to the motel. For the next few days Wayne taught me how to play bass.

On the floor: Charlie McCoy, Ray Knowles: Bass, Snuffy Smith and a girl

Kent & Snuffy – MGM Records promo

Tex Ritter: with Kent on bass

Carl Perkins – center w/hat. Louie Stewart left – Kent and Clayton Perkins, Carl's brother – Boulder Dam

Kent, left. Wayne Gray – Billy Sprout Cosby, at the Nevada Club – Las Vegas – on tour with Tex Ritter.

Tex Ritter, far right: Kent. Billy Sprout Cosby
and Wayne Gray in Vietnam –'67

Chapter 10

BACK AND FORTH WITH TEX

*W*hen we got back to town, Jimmy Day - a great steel guitar player and old runnin' buddy of mine – told me he had a Silvertone bass that he'd sell me for fifty bucks. I bought it and a cheap bass amp. That got me by for the next few months. Then I got lucky. On our next tour with Tex, Leo Fender, owner of Fender Guitar Company, told us to come by. He outfitted us with *all new Fender equipment*. I got a brand new Fender bass and Fender amp!

We were backstage one night at a high school auditorium on tour. Tex, Wayne, and I, along with Jean Shepard and some others, were sitting back there when Ernie Ashworth, who had a big hit with a song titled "Talk Back Tremblin' Lips" walked by wearing his embroidered "Lips" suit. Jean quipped, "It's a good thing he didn't have a hit on Mr. Peters." Everyone fell out.

All that Glitters: Tex, Wayne, Billy, and I were working Jackpot, Nevada. Between shows, Wayne, Billy, and I drove around. Down the highway a few miles we found a little town called Contact, Nevada - nothing much there but a gas station and a convenience store. There was a dirt road that led into the mountains. We drove up there and came across some old mining shafts. Hmm, we thought, could be interesting. We got out of the car and looked around. We spotted several rocks, each with a shiny glittering vein going through it. Immediately, we thought we'd found gold! We put several of these rocks into Tex's car and hurried back to the motel. On the sidewalk in front of the motel, we hammered away at the gleaming lines in the rocks. Tex came out and asked, "What are you doing, boys?" We told him we thought we'd found gold. Tex started laughing. He said, "Boys! What you have there is *mica*, fool's gold. It's not worth anything." That ended our treasure hunting.

Two doors down from Cedarwood on Music Row was a beer joint called the Country Corner. A big bunch of writers and artists used to frequent the place in the afternoons. Faron Young, George Jones, Billy Swan, Billy Joe Shaver, and Eddie Miller (writer of "Release Me," "There She Goes," "Playboy" and many other songs) would be there. Also, sometimes you could see Terry Fell (singer and writer of "Truck Drivin' Man"), Ed Bruce, Wayne Kemp, Wayne Walker, Leon Ashley, and Doodle Owens (who later co-wrote "Wine-Colored Roses", "The Bird" for George Jones, and many other hits). There were lots of others.

Across the street from Columbia Studios was the Tally Ho Tavern - later the name was changed to the Professional Club or Wally's Club. Whatever the name, they served stronger drinks. That was one of our watering holes. Another frequent hangout was the Boar's Nest, a small apartment belonging to Sue Brewer, who catered to artists and writers. Webb Pierce, George Jones, Faron Young, and others would go there and play darts, sing their songs, and drink beer. There was also Big Dot's Place, named for the female member of the Smokey and Dot duet team of earlier country music history.

Jack D. Johnson was employed by Cedarwood as a public relations man. Jack and I would hang out from time to time. One afternoon, Jack got a tape and phone call from a country singer from Montana. His name was Charlie Pride. Jack liked what he heard and then found out the singer was Black. Jack thought, "He sure doesn't sound Black." He played the tape for Jack "Cowboy" Clement, who played it for Chet Atkins. In short order, Charlie was signing an RCA contract. He quickly made musical history, becoming the first Black country star, or should I say, superstar!

By then Cedarwood had moved out to Music Row across the street from Columbia Studios. Jim Denny's widow (Miss Dollie, as everyone called her) was the front secretary at Cedarwood. Everyone loved her. I first met Merv Shiner at Cedarwood. He was dating Miss Dollie and would stop by a lot. Merv recorded the million-selling hit "Here Comes Peter Cottontail." Although he recorded many other country records, none would surpass "Cottontail." Merv and I became close friends and wrote quite a few songs together, including "I've Got Yesterday" cut by Kitty Wells and "If You Had Only Taken the Time" recorded by Charlie Pride.

"Minnie Pearl" (Ophelia Colley) used to come in to visit with Miss Dollie. They were good friends. She was such a nice lady. I was introduced to her. She asked where I was from and how long I'd been in Nashville and stuff like that. She never forgot my name.

Shootout in Ole Nashville: Darrell McCall and I were still sharing a duplex. One night we didn't have anything to do so we dressed up in cowboy outfits, strapped on guns, spurs, cowboy hats - the whole nine yards - and went downtown. We got to Linebaugh's and Darrell said, "Give me five seconds, then you come in shooting." It was on a Saturday night and the place was packed. Darrell *threw* open the doors, *drew* his pistol, *rushed* over to the last booth and *ducked* down. I ran in right after him, guns drawn and yelling, "BANG! BANG!" Everyone dropped their silverware and whatever else in disbelief. Management was not amused. As a result of our dramatic duo, Darrell and I were barred and told not to ever come back. In a couple of weeks, however, all was forgiven, and we were able to go back in.

Don Rich and Doyle Holly worked in Buck Owens' band. We would pal around together on the road. We were on a lot of package shows together. Don was later killed in a motorcycle accident in 1974.

Holy Guacamole! Another time Tex, Wayne, and I were working out West. I was driving. About two in the morning we were coming into Tombstone, Arizona. I saw a sign that said Boot Hill Cemetery. *Oh man, Sally, tell your sister!* I was crazy about Old West history. Tex was still snoring in the front seat. I shook Wayne awake and said in a loud whisper, "Wayne, *Boot Hill Cemetery!*" There was a fence and gate with a sign that said, "Closed." Wayne was also a history nut. We left Tex asleep in the front seat, climbed the fence, and started clambering over graves with cigarette lighters, trying to see who was buried where. I stood on Three-Fingered Jack's grave - he was right-hand man to the notorious *bandito*, Joaquin Murrieta. In the Old West, Joaquin had been known as the "Robin Hood of California." I couldn't believe I had been lucky enough to find that grave! We finally got back into the car and continued on down the road. Tex was still snoring.

In Nashville, Tex was asked to play the grand opening of the movie *Your Cheatin' Heart,* the story of Hank Williams starring George Hamilton, at the Tennessee Theater. It was like a Hollywood premiere. I got to meet Susan Oliver who played Audrey Williams, and Arthur O'Connell who played the part of Fred Rose. I loved the movie. It was said that Audrey didn't like it.

Chapter 11

JOHNNY CASH,
THE STATLERS, AND CUBA

A short time later, Tex became a member of the Johnny Cash package show. We went everywhere Johnny went. One time The Tennessee Three's van broke down. Wayne, Billy, and I filled in and backed Johnny. I remember we had to tune all our instruments up one-half a key from standard tuning. That's so Cash could play in the key of "E" position. Normally we played in the standard key of "F."

I recall one afternoon at a fair date in Staunton, Virginia, The Statler Brothers came up and asked Johnny if they could audition for him. He put them on the show that afternoon and later took them with him to Nashville. Johnny was instrumental in getting them on Columbia. None of their last names was Statler, so I asked Don Reid, one of the group, how they came by their name. Don said they had been trying to think of a name when they noticed a matchbook cover on the desk of the hotel they were staying in. It said "Statler Hotel." They all liked the name. That's how we got The Statler Brothers.

Batty About the Guy: The Statlers were big fans of the *Batman* TV series when it first came out in the 1960s. We'd be driving to the next date and, no matter where we were when it came time for a Batman episode, The Statlers would pull over, check into the first motel they came to, and watch the show. Then they'd turn around, check out, and continue on down the road.

Johnny's lead guitar player, Luther Perkins, and I used to sit out in Luther's and wife Margie's camper between shows and play songs to each other. I loved Luther. Most people didn't know that his brother was Thomas Wayne, who had the rock and roll hit "Tragedy" in 1959. Later, I was sad to hear that Luther had been burned to death in a fire started when a lit cigarette caught the couch on fire where he was sleeping. Marshall Grant was Johnny's bass player and W.S. "Fluky" Holland was Johnny's drummer. Fluky was Carl Perkins' drummer in the beginning. Carl Perkins took Luther's place playing lead guitar for Johnny after Luther's passing.

Cash had such charisma when he was on stage, you couldn't take your eyes off him. On many a show, Wayne, Billy, and I used to go out and just sit in the audience and watch him. It was around this time that June Carter joined the show. It was on one of these shows that Johnny asked June to marry him. She did.

Sometime after our Cash connection ended, we were supposed to play for a Boy Scouts of America function in Key West, Florida. Tex was going to fly down on this particular trip, and we were going to meet him at the airport in Miami. We drove down there and got to the airport, only to find that Tex's flight had been hijacked to Cuba! Ironically, we had joked about that very thing on the way down. We could hardly believe it. We figured the best thing to do was to go on down and do the show for the Boy Scouts anyway. We drove to Key West and did the show, explaining to the audience what had happened to Tex. Then we drove back to the airport and waited. Finally, Tex got there - madder than a hornet! Then we all rode back to Nashville.

I stayed with Tex for a little over three years. He was like a father to all of us. Before Billy had joined us on drums, I remember Tex living in California where he had bought Cecil B. DeMille's house. Wayne and I had to drive from Nashville to California to pick him up. We stayed in the apartment above the swimming pool where Tex kept all his saddles and other memorabilia from his acting days.

We were riding along in the car one day, and I asked Tex what Hank Williams was like. Tex said that once he and Hank were on a plane together, and Tex asked, "Hank, how come you never cut one of my songs?"

Hank replied, "You never cut one of mine." They made a deal to record one of each other's songs. Tex recorded "You're Barking Up the Wrong Tree Now," which did nothing at all. Hank recorded Tex's song "Dear John (I Sent your Saddle Home)," which was a big hit for Hank.

When I left Cedarwood I had about 400 songs recorded there and was still working with Tex. We had a string of dates across the whole length of Canada. We started out in Toronto and ended up in New Brunswick, British Columbia.

Slick as a Whistle: I remember I was driving somewhere in the middle of Canada about seventy mph on a highway in the winter, and up ahead it looked like a perfect straight line across the highway where the road pavement changed color. It was black ice! We hit it and started spinning. We must have spun at least four times. I noticed a three-foot embankment on the roadside. I knew we were going to go right into it and, if we did, we were going to get stuck. I gave it the gas and steered right for the embankment, went in, and turned the wheel all the way to the left. I had enough momentum to climb right back up on the road and then I stopped. Tex woke up and said, "Are we there yet?"

I said, "No, Tex, we're just changing drivers."

Cindy Walker was one of country music's best-known songwriters. She had written such songs as "Bubbles in My Beer" recorded by Bob Wills and others, "Cherokee Maiden" by Merle Haggard and others,

"You Don't Know Me" by Eddy Arnold, "In the Misty Moonlight" by Jerry Wallace and others, "Distant Drums" by Jim Reeves, and hundreds more songs. She lived with her mother in Mexia, Texas. Well, Tex and all of us were playing in Texas, and Cindy invited us over to her house for a picnic lunch. We went over to her house one afternoon and had a picnic in her backyard. That was great. What a talented lady she was.

Just a Splash Here and There: On one of our trips to California to pick up Tex, Wayne and I were shopping at a drug store. They had a huge display of English Leather aftershave cologne in a one-gallon bottle. I asked the lady if she would sell the display bottle. She said for thirty-five dollars she would. I bought it. For the next fourteen years I think I smelled pretty nice.

Shortly after that, Tex and his wife, Dorothy, moved to Nashville. Tommy, his youngest son, came too. Tommy had cerebral palsy when he was young and still had a slight limp. He became a good lawyer and now lives in California. Tex's oldest son, John, traveled with us one whole summer while he was on vacation from acting school in England. They both were great guys.

Right to the Point: One afternoon Tex went to the doctor's office to get a shot for something or other. The nurse came in with a loaded syringe. Tex glared at it and said, "Miss, do you know you're about to stick that needle in *America's most beloved cowboy's ass?'*

Chapter 12

MUSIC CITY AND ELSEWHERE

Back in Nashville, I met Dorsey Burnette in Tootsie's. Dorsey was Johnny Burnette's brother. They both came out of The Johnny Burnette Trio from the 1950s. Johnny had a lot of hits on his own, and so did Dorsey. Dorsey wrote a lot of songs for Ricky Nelson. We hung around together for a few days while I introduced him to the town.

Audrey Williams, Hank's wife, had an office across the street from Cedarwood. Merle Kilgore was manager. He also managed Hank Jr. Merle was also a great writer. He had written "Ring of Fire" for Johnny Cash with June Carter, and Webb Pierce's "More and More," a big hit in the 1950s. Merle wrote "Wolverton Mountain" for Claude King and others. Anyway, I had this song that Benny Joy and I had just written called "Help Me Up, Darlin' (All Fools Fall Down)." I took a copy over to Merle and he loved it. He had a single on it.

At the time, I was dating a girl named Diana. One night we were over at my place and she started singing. She was really good. I arranged a demo session and had her sing three of my songs: "He's Like a Cold Cup of Coffee (He's Not So Hot)," "Side Street," and "Time Have Mercy on Me." They came off great. I took them over to Billy Graves, Capitol Records' A&R man. I might note that Billy was half of The Country Lads with Dick Flood, who was earlier on the *Jimmy Dean Show Town* and *Country Time*. Billy liked what he heard. He said he thought Capitol would sign her. I went back to Cedarwood and told Bill Denny, who had taken over after Jim died. Bill said, "Let me put her out on Dollie Records." Dollie had signed Carl Perkins and other artists. I said OK. They changed Diana's last name to Duke. Now she was Diana Duke. The records didn't do much, but as luck would have it, Diana married Larry Williams, a drummer, and that changed her name to Diana Williams. Capitol signed her anyway, and she had a hit with "Teddy Bear's Last Ride," the answer to Red Sovine's big hit "Teddy Bear."

It was there that I wrote and recorded "Married to a Jukebox" backed with "I Sent You Me." It came out on JED Records. Lloyd Green later said it was one of the first sessions he played steel guitar on. About this time my contract was up with Cedarwood and I left. I ran into Jimmy Day at Tootsie's one night. He was working with Pete Drake and his publishing company, Window Music. We were sitting around having a few beers, and Jimmy said, "Let's go pick someplace. Have you got any songs?" I said yes. He got on the phone and called up a few musicians, and we all went out to Starday studios. Tommy Hill was the engineer. Tommy had written the hit song "Slowly" for Webb Pierce years before. Tommy was also the brother of Goldie Hill, a top country artist married to Carl Smith.

Bob-Bob-Bobbin': I got to thinking about the old joke about the two robins sitting up in this tree looking down on this farmer's field at all the worms below. One robin turned to the other and said, "Let's go down and have some lunch," so they flew down and ate the worms. They were so full, and the sun was so warm they rolled around till they fell asleep. Two cats were sitting on the fence watching. One cat turned to the other and said, "Let's go down and have some lunch." They went down and ate the two birds. One cat turned to the other and said, "I just love *baskin' robins.*"

I remember I was putting a crazy song down called "I'm a Blue-bird" about a bird's-eye view of the world from a bird's perspective. Just to show you what I mean, here are the first two verses:

> Spring comes, flowers bloom,
> people are singing all out of tune
> Tweet tweet, ain't I sweet
> Ha ha ha I'm a bluebird
> Sittin' high in a big oak tree
> Lookin' at the people lookin' at me
> Chirp, chirp, ain't I absurd
> Ha ha ha I'm a blue bird.

Harold Morrison recorded the song.

I noticed George Hamilton IV had come in with this girl and was talking to Tommy in the engineer's booth. She was pretty, but I didn't think anything of it. A short time later, I got a call from Patsy Stoneman. She asked me if I would play bass and open the show for her at the Western Room in Printer's Alley. She was going to be there for a week. I said okay. I was playing on stage one night when Porter Wagoner came in with the same girl I had seen in the studio with George Hamilton IV. I went over and said hello. She said, "Do you always rock back and forth like that, honey?" I was insulted. I didn't like her. I had met the love of my life but didn't know it yet!

It's IMPORTANT that I mention this here: I was close to God, but I didn't live like it. I got sidetracked a lot. Still, I was praying real hard for a girl that I could fall in love with and who I would want to marry.

What's in a Kiss? A few weeks went by. I was out "roaring" (as they called it then) with Kris Kristofferson, another pal of mine. We went into Linebaugh's and saw two girls sitting at a table. Kris waved at them and they waved back. I said, "Do you know them?"

He said, "Yeah, do you want to meet them?"

I said, "Yeah. Who's the dark-haired girl?"

He said, "That's Dale Turner from Washington, DC, and the other one is Pat McKinney. Both are good singers." Kris introduced us. It didn't register that Dale had been the girl I had seen at the studio with George, or the one I later saw with Porter. I asked her if she'd like to go to a movie sometime. She said yes.

A few weeks went by. I called her, and we had our first date. I was a little on the shy side and didn't try to kiss her. She said, "Aren't you going to kiss me goodnight?" I did. She told me later that she never felt so much peace after that kiss going home. That was the Lord. I know that.

We used to date each other's girls. I told all the guys, "Hands off this one. Dale and I are going steady!" Dale and Kris were good friends, and Dale said to Kris, "He's kinda weird and rocks back and forth. What kind of guy is he?" Kris stuck up for me and even wrote a song about it. He told Dale, "I'd rather be sorry for something I've done than something I didn't do." He told Dale you won't know until you try.

One afternoon I bought two steaks and drove to Dale's house. I decided to cook us up some great steaks. She answered the door with no make-up on and her hair up in curlers. I thought WOW she sure looks different, still pretty, though.

Dale had been one of Patsy Cline's closest friends in Washington, DC, and was at the wedding when Patsy married Charlie Dick. They were together on the *Jimmy Dean Show Town* and *Country Time*. The stage was built on a wooden platform. Dale remembered that, during the filming of one of the shows, when they called everyone out at the end to sing the closing song, "Riding down to Santa Fe," there were about twenty people on the stage. It started sinking. Everyone went running for their lives!

Patsy had an earlier hit, "Walking after Midnight," in the late fifties. Before moving to Nashville, Patsy was called to do the Alan Freed Show in New York. Mr. Freed was one of the nation's top rock and roll DJs and show promoters at the time. Patsy called Dale and asked her to go with her. She did. Patsy later recorded "I Fall to Pieces" and "Crazy," among many other hits. Tragically, she died in a plane crash in 1963.

It was about this time that Dale landed a Columbia Records contract, and Bob Tubert produced her session. She cut four songs. One of them was mine. She also recorded one of Dolly Parton's songs and one by Bob Tubert and Demetris Tapp titled "False Eyelashes."

Dale and Pat McKinney lived in Donelson, a suburb of Nashville, and I had moved in with Snuffy, who was divorced by then. We also lived with P.J. Babcock, a drummer with little Jimmy Dickens' Band, at the Madison Square Apartments in Madison, Tennessee.

John Hartford lived right across the hall from us. John and I were pretty good friends. He was writing for Tompall and The Glaser Bros. Publishing Company when he wrote "Gentle On My Mind." Enough said!

Dale had two daughters by a previous marriage, and they came home for the summer. They had been away to school. Judy was the youngest at six, and Susan was eleven.

Dale and the kids would come over and use the swimming pool a lot. It was right about then I asked Dale to marry me. She agreed, and we set the date that September 7th because that was my mom and dad's wedding anniversary (and my parents' marriage had lasted all these years).

Everyone at Tootsies' was placing bets we wouldn't make it six months. We made it fifty-two years so far and still going. That was in '67. I remember Tootsie came to our wedding, and so did Tom T. Hall. They were there among many other friends. Of course, Tom T. Hall wrote "Old Dogs and Children and Watermelon Wine", "Harper Valley P.T.A.", and "I'm not Ready Yet."

At this point, I'm still working with Tex, and we were working the Opry some. We also worked the WWVA Wheeling, West Virginia, hayride, and The Big D Jamboree in Dallas, Texas. Tex was asked to co-host the *Ralph Emery Radio Show*, and Wayne and I would go up there with Tex from time to time. Ralph would refer to me as the "Rocking One," and Tex as "America's Most Beloved Cowboy." Tex had made well over fifty Western movies.

I was between publishers. In other words, I didn't have one, but I was still writing. I was by myself working on a song called "Be Glad (You Got Whatcha Got when You Got It, or You're Gonna Find That What You Got is Gone)." I had a verse and chorus written when somebody knocked at the door. It was Justin Tubb. He said, "Whatcha doin?" I played him what I had on the song. He liked it, and we finished it. He left a little while later. I called Buddy Killen at Tree Publishing Company and asked him if I could do a demo session for Tree. He said, "When do you want to do it?" I told him soon and that I had about four songs. He set it up right away. I put the four songs down. "Be Glad" was one of them. More about this later.

Jack "Cowboy" Clement, Kris Kristofferson, and I were at the Tally Ho Tavern one night. Kris told Jack that I was looking for a place and he needed to sign me as a writer. Jack told me to come see him the next day. Thanks to Kris, he signed me to a writer's contract with Jack Music, Inc. Jack Clement was the recording engineer with Sun Records and Sam Phillips in the fifties. Jack also wrote and recorded many hits himself, to name a few: "Ballad of a Teenage Queen" for Johnny Cash, "Miller's Cave" for Hank Snow, and "Just Between You and Me" by Charlie Pride. Among some of the other writers with Jack were Vince Matthews, Bob McDill, ("Amanda," "Song of the South," "Gone Country," "Louisiana Saturday Night" and others), Jerry Foster and Bill Rice. Even though they wrote for Hall-Clement, Jack still owned half the publishing. Jack liked Dale's singing and asked her if she would sing a Foster and Rice song. She did the original demo on "The Easy Part's Over Now," the Charlie Pride hit.

These were the times when artists and songwriters used to pal around with each other. Dallas Frazier was a good friend and one of the top songwriters of the day – or any other day. He wrote "Alley Oop" by The Hollywood Argyles as a teenager. Later he also had hits like "Elvira," "There Goes My Everything," "All I Have to Offer You is Me", among others. He came from California and settled in Nashville. More about him later.

I ran into Merle Travis at Cedarwood one afternoon, and he asked me if I would open for Joe Maphis and Rose Lee the following week and play bass in Printer's Alley, at the Western Room. I said sure. I worked with them for a week. I had a ball.

Vince Matthews, a writer with Jack Music, used to come over a lot, as well as a new writer/singer named Eddie Rabbitt. Eddie and I wrote a couple of songs that never got recorded. Eddie later became a hit writer and artist. Doug Kershaw would drop in from time to time. One night, Vince Matthews came over, and I told him I had this idea about a middle-aged man looking out of a window in an undershirt overlooking a square in Louisiana. I had a title: "Love in The Hot Afternoon." We wrote it inside of an hour. Then Vince said, "I have this song I'm working on called 'She Simply Left (and After That She Was Gone)'." We wrote it that same night. Mac Wiseman later recorded that one. Come to find out they had made a mistake in the pressing and forgot to put my name on it as a writer. However, I got paid on it, and they corrected the mistake on future pressings.

I moved in with Dale in Donelson, and Pat moved out. Pat didn't like me much then, but we came to love each other as brother and sister. Pat is very talented as a singer and performer. She recorded for Mega Records and worked constantly on package shows with many top artists. Pat later was "Miss Sarah" on the *General Jackson Showboat* for twelve years.

Around that time Eddie Miller, Buddy Mize, music-business secretary Maggie Cavender, and others started the Nashville Songwriters Association. Dale was on the first board of directors, and I did research for nominees to the Songwriters Hall of Fame. I was on the board for two years and did all the other research for it.

Dale and I bought our first house on Moyna Drive in Hendersonville, Tennessee. We bought our carpet from a guy named Hal Harbour who worked at the only carpet store in town. Come to find out, Hal was a songwriter too. We became fast friends and started writing some together. More about him later.

I recall when I had just demoed two duet songs, one I had written with Dale called "What We Used to Hang On to is Gone" and "Party People," one that Hal Harbour and I wrote. Bob Webster, a pitchman for Jack Music, sent both of them to Hank Williams Jr, who was looking for a girl singer to sing duets with at the time. Lois Johnson and Jerry Monday, dobro player with The Stonemans, did the original demo. Hank Jr. called the company and asked who the girl on the demo was. He wanted her for his duet partner. He recorded both songs. They were both singles.

Jack Clement was producing a movie in Nashville called *Dear Dead Delilah* with Agnes Morehead. It was her last film before she passed away. I was an extra in it, along with Dickie Lee and a bunch of other writers. It took about four hours just to shoot the ten seconds I was in - just a lot of sitting around waiting on the cameras. Dale and I were also extras in the Burt Reynolds film *W.W. and the Dixie Dance Kings*. We were in the dance scene in the high school gym. We were also in *Framed* with Joe Don Baker. We had lunch with Joe Don, a very nice man. Joe Don also starred as Buford Pusser in the movie *Walking Tall*. We did a cerebral palsy telethon with the real Buford and had lunch with him a couple of times. He was a big guy, six-foot-six. He had been sheriff of a small town in Tennessee who set out to rid the town of gangsters who had taken over some of the local clubs. He'd been wounded several times, but that didn't stop him. He finally was killed in an auto accident going at a high rate of speed. They think someone had tampered with the brakes.

DALE TURNER

featured with
THE JIMMY CASE SHOW

Dale Turner Columbia Records photo.

Dale Turner and Patsy Cline – at the Alan Freed Show.

Dale Turner, Jimmy Case and the Cherokee's band..

The Jimmy Dean show – cast. – Town & Country Time – Dale Turner
Center: Connie B. Gay, Center Back: Left Center: Jimmy Dean: and cast

Patsy Cline's autographed picture to Dale.

Top left: Buck Ryan, Mary Klick, Jimmy Dean, Dale Turner,
Marvin Carroll, Bottom: Alex Houston & Eumer, Billy Grammar,
Smitty Irvin, Herbie Jones.

Dale and Patsy: at Patsy's wedding to Charlie Dick.

Chapter 13

VIETNAM, TEXAS, AND DEL REEVES

I believe it was around 1967 when Tex, Wayne, Billy, and I went on tour overseas to Vietnam to entertain the troops. That's the first time I met Jimmy Case, our booking agent. Jimmy Case was an entertainer too. His band was The Cherokees, and Dale, my wife, traveled with his show back in DC before moving to Nashville.

A Little too Close for Comfort: We were staying in Saigon at a hotel, and a bus driver would drive us to where we were playing in an old bus. In one place we played, they were bringing in the wounded in helicopters and laying them out on the ground in front of us. After the show on the way back, we were stopped by armed soldiers. I don't know if they were Vietcong or Vietnamese troops. They ordered us off the bus at gunpoint. The driver was explaining to the soldiers that we were Tex Ritter and band, that Tex was a cowboy movie star, and that we had nothing to do with the war. After a while they let us get back on the bus. We went back to the hotel. *WHEW!!!*

In the stillness of the night you could hear howitzer shells buzzing overhead and the explosions when they hit, even though it could be miles away. You could feel the walls shake. We were in a helicopter at one point going to another place. The machine-gunner right in back of me looked to be not more than seventeen years old. The chopper door was open, and we could see puffs of smoke coming from beneath us. Tex said "What are they doing down there?"

The pilot said, "They're shooting at us, Tex, but they can't hit us from there. They only have 22-millimeter guns."

Tex said, "Would you mind closing the door? It's getting a little drafty in here!" We all laughed.

We were over there for about three or four weeks, then on to Taiwan for a week. It felt like I hadn't seen Dale in forever. We finally got back home. I quit Tex to be at home more often and do more writing. I think Snuffy took my place with Tex.

Just Don't Mess with My Guitar: I was still on draw at Jack Music making seventy-five bucks a week. It wasn't much. Dale and I formed our own band, got a booking agent, and started working clubs. We got booked in Texas at a club called Dale's Blue Lounge. We were there only a week, but it felt like two. We had a matinee in the afternoon. I guess I'd had too many drinks before the night show. On one of our breaks, a certain cowboy who had been giving Dale the eye had un-tuned my guitar. I was hoppin' mad! Over the mic I invited "the coward who'd done that dirty deed" to step outside. Half the club sided with me, and the other half sided with the cowboy. There was a big fight about it. When I went to get paid, the owner said, "I guess you know you won't be back."

A couple of weeks later we worked Mason City, Iowa. That was a lot better gig. On our way back to Nashville, we were listening to the *Ralph Emery Show*, and Del Reeves was his guest. He played Del's new record. It was "Be Glad," the song I had written with Justin Tubb. We were thrilled! When we got back to Nashville, we found out that some guy by the name of R. Richardson claimed to be the writer of it. His name was on the first pressings of the record. I called Buddy Killen at Tree. Buddy got it straightened out. All future pressings were corrected. It seems that this guy came to Nashville, got hold of a demo of the song, took it to another publisher, and got an advance on it. The song eventually went to number one in *Record World*, number two in *Cashbox*, and number three in the Billboard charts.

Del Reeves was a great guy and entertainer. We did a lot of shows with him. He could impersonate just about everybody on the Opry – he'd sound just like them. He also was a practical joker. Sometimes he would walk out on stage while we were in the middle of a song with a bag over his head and clown around.

One Step at a Time: One day the guys in the band and I decided to turn the tables on Del. We went to the Goodwill store in the town where we were playing and bought the biggest pair of shoes we could find. They happened to be *pink and green, two-toned, perforated shoes.* We knew that, in the middle of Del's show, he did a medley of old country songs that always included "My Shoes Keep Walking Back to You." We got to the show early, tied fishing line to the shoes, and put them on the far side of the stage. When Del started singing "My Shoes Keep Walking Back to You," we started pulling the shoes one at a time across the front of the stage. When they got in front of Del, he lost it. That was funny!!!

On the home front, we worked the Western Room in Printer's Alley a lot and were on the road quite a bit too. Dale's two girls, Judy and Susan, were living with us now. They loved the band rehearsals and the writers coming over. There were people like Billy Joe Shaver, Red Lane, Eddie Rabbitt, "Handsome" Harlan Sanders, Mack Vickery, Tom Ghent, and others.

I want to interject this here because it's very important: earlier, I had prayed to the Lord for a girl that I could fall in love with and marry. Well, he answered my prayer. He sent me Dale! In return, I told the Lord, "I'll go to church every Sunday from now on." I've tried to do that. Also, I told Dale we were going to tithe ten percent of everything we made from then on. Not only that, but I would never let it fall below twenty-five dollars a week, whether we made it or not (we still do that today). It wasn't long after I made that commitment that we had checks coming in from everywhere! My BMI royalty checks tripled, I got checks from some radio recording service, our road dates increased. The Lord blessed us mightily!

It was about this time I got word that DeBeaux, my daughter from my previous marriage to Grace, wasn't faring well. Dale and I drove down to Miami, went to court, and fought for her custody. We won. We moved her up to Tennessee with us. Now we were a complete family.

A lot of times, the kids would have their friends over, playing softball in the back yard. I'd stick my head out the door, and the kids would holler, "Hey Dad, what's for dinner!?" In my best and loudest Hee-Haw voice - impersonating Grandpa Jones - I'd reply, "Well, we're having collard greens and possum stew, coffee hot and corn bread too – *YUM! YUM!*" Everyone would fall out laughing.

I would spend a lot of my time downtown on Music Row, writing and drinking and trying to pitch songs. I would shoot pool with a lot of my friends, like Faron Young, Ed Bruce, Wayne Kemp, and others.

For a brief period, I went to work with Dick Flood playing bass, who at this time was married to Pat McKinney. His group was called The Pathfinders. Dick was a fine entertainer and songwriter. He started out as half of The Country Lads with Billy Graves before going on his own. He later wrote The Wilburn Brothers hit, "Trouble's Back in Town." A few years later, Dick and Pat broke up and Dick became "Okefenokee Joe," a swamp guide in Georgia.

Where's my Morning Paper? Red Lane (Hollis DeLaughter) would come over to the house every now and then and hang out with us. Red was another writer friend. He wrote "Country Girl" by Dottie West, "Till I Get It Right" by Tammy Wynette, and "My Own Kind of Hat" by Merle Haggard, just to name a few. Red also wanted to record for RCA, so he devised a plan. He went over one night to the house of Chet Atkins (an A&R man for RCA Records and great guitar player) and pitched a tent in Chet's front yard. The next morning Chet went out to get his morning paper, and there was Red. Chet said, "What are you doing out here?"

Red said, "I want to record for RCA."

Chet said, "Okay, if you'll move your tent off my front yard." Red recorded an LP for RCA called "The World Needs a Melody." He bought an old airplane, fixed it up inside, and lived in it. He was a little on the eccentric side.

Our house was a split-level with a nice, big den on the bottom floor. We lived there for about seven years. A funny thing: I was out mowing the yard one afternoon on the side of the house. We had already lived there about four years. I passed by a window with curtains hanging there. It dawned on me: there was no window inside the house there! I got off the lawnmower, went inside, and looked. Nope, no window. After four years or so, I finally noticed it. Someone had built a brick wall over the window and left the curtains hanging there. There for a second, I thought I had entered the Twilight Zone!

On Sundays the kids would go to Sunday school. I'd pick them up. They remember a few times they'd be out front, waving and jumping up and down and watching me sail right on by them. It would dawn on me about half a block later that I was supposed to pick them up! Probably thinking of a song or something. I'd turn around and go back for them. When we got home they couldn't wait to tell Dale, "Dad forgot us again!"

One afternoon on Music Row I ran into Doyle Wilburn of The Wilburn Brothers. Doyle told me that Bob Wills and The Texas Playboys had just recorded one of my songs for Kapp Records. It was a single, "She Won't Let Me Forget Her (She's Afraid that I Will)." Jody Nix also recorded that one, an old song Snuffy and I had written in 1960 when we were staying at the YMCA. Surefire Music had publishing on it. It was owned by The Wilburns. I was so proud that Bob Wills would do one of my songs. Yep, life was good.

Rockin' 'Round the Cop: I was pretty good friends with Dean (Pee Wee) Mathis, one of The New Beats who had the hit song "Bread and Butter," among others. One night on my way to Printer's Alley I saw Pee Wee stumbling out of the Western Room. To say he was tipsy is putting it mildly. He said, "I can't find my car."

I said, "I'll help you find it." We walked down the street. There were several parking lots. We came to a corner where we stopped, waiting for the red light to change. I was rocking back and forth. A police car screeched up to where we were. The cop threw me in the back seat. Pee Wee turned and wobbled back to the Western Room. They took me downtown to night court. The cop told the judge he thought I was drunk because I was weaving back and forth. I told the judge I hadn't even had a beer. After explaining to the judge about my rocking habit that I had all my life, he dismissed the case.

Getting off on the Wrong Foot: One of the most embarrassing moments I ever had was when Dale and I went to the movies and saw *Raiders of the Lost Ark* when it first came out. The theater was packed, and the only two seats left were smack dab in the middle of the center section. The movie had just started when we maneuvered our way to the seats. No more had we got there and sat down when Dale said, "I got to have some popcorn." I thought to myself, OH NO! I started to get up and my foot stepped on something gooey and slid right out from under me! I fell into the lady's lap next to me, and the more I tried to get my footing, the more I slid. I ended up on the lap of the guy sitting next to her! They tried to help lift me up. With no small commotion, I got to my feet and worked my way out into the aisle. I made it up to the concession stand and got the popcorn. I was almost too embarrassed to go back in. It was too dark to see, and I had forgotten to count the rows to where we were sitting. I started down the aisle down to where I thought I was getting close. Then I heard someone say, "Look out, here he comes again!" Finally I got seated again. Whew!! I still remember that to this day.

Printer's Alley had about four or five clubs all next door to each other: the Western Room, the Black Poodle, and several others. History has it that Andrew Jackson used to ride down there and tie his horse to one of the hitching posts in front of the print shops where the clubs are now. We got to know several of the managers of the Western Room. "Cadillac" was one. We never knew his real name. Everyone just called him Cadillac. "Skull" was another one. It was Skull that took us upstairs over the Western Room one night and showed us some rooms that had been closed up for years. They used to be gambling places back in the day. It was said that Jesse James had frequented them on many occasions.

Chapter 14

THE WILLEX DAYS

Dale was working the Alley in the Western Room, and I was booked on a date for a Willex party. Willex was like Amway. They had all kinds of products like soap, cosmetics, and cleaners. My band was called The Memory Makers, named after the song "Memory Maker" that I had written with Mel Tillis, which was a hit in 1975. We went over so well that Mike Peavyhouse, the head of Willex, came over and asked us to play some more shows for them. I took Dale with me on the next show and they loved us. Mike said, "How would you like to work all our shows exclusively?" He put us on a salary of five hundred dollars a week whether we worked or not. Back then that was good money. He gave us an expense account and a new Cadillac to drive. It was great! All our gas was taken care of, hotel expenses, everything. On our next Willex show date, we took the kids. While we were doing the show, they ran up four hundred dollars worth of expenses for room service and I don't know what all. But it was all taken care of. They had a blast!

Then Mike Peavyhouse wanted to start a record label called Willex Records, and he wanted me to do the producing. I got back to Nashville and started the ball rolling. We went first class right on down the line. The top session players were on our recordings. They included Buddy Emmons on bass and steel, Jimmy Capps on lead, Jeff Newman on steel, Buddy Harmon and Kenny Malone on drums, and Tommy Jackson and Buddy Spicher on fiddles. We recorded at the major studios.

Hal Harbour and I were still writing some great songs. At that time Mel Tillis and Sherry Bryce were doing duets. They recorded three of Hal's and my songs: "Mr. Right and Mrs. Wrong," "You are the One," and "Two Strangers Passing in the Night." All three of them were singles. Mel recorded a song Hal and I wrote called "Thank You for Being You," which I dedicated to my wife Dale, my inspiration. Also Mel cut "Pictures," another song Hal and I wrote.

My first record on Willex was "God, Country, Apple Pie, Willex, and You," sort of a commercial on one side. The other side was "Back in Seattle Again," a takeoff on the old Gene Autry song, "Back in the Saddle Again." Our second artist for the label was, of course, my wife, Dale Turner - my favorite girl singer. Her first single was "Happy Honkin', Honky Tonkin' Truck Driving Man" backed by "Love Rings an Old Bell with Me." "Happy Honkin'" got a lot of play in Texas. Dale and I recorded several duets for the label including "Forget There Ever Was a Yesterday" and "Mr. Right and Mrs. Wrong."

Dale's second single for the label was "Same Old Song and Dance" backed by "Three Little Memories." I might add that my daughter, Susan, sang harmony with Dale on that record.

Then we did a show for Willex in Omaha, Nebraska. A young fellow by the name of Max D. Barnes came backstage and wanted us to hear some songs he wrote. After hearing them, I knew he was a good songwriter and needed to be in Nashville. Max and I wrote several songs together. Max was also a great singer. A few weeks later I brought him to Nashville, and he stayed with us for a while till he could move his family down.

I produced Max's first session for the Willex label, "You Gotta Be Putting Me On," backed by a song he and I wrote, "Growing Old with

Grace." Later on, Max wrote such hits as "Chiseled in Stone" for Vern Gosdin, "Who's Gonna Fill Their Shoes?" by George Jones, "Redneckin,' Love Makin' Night" for Conway Twitty, "Look at Us" with Vince Gill, "Thank God for the Radio" by The Kendalls, and many more hits. Note: Max had recorded "Ribbons of Steel" a few years earlier for the JED label on his first trip to Nashville. It got some notable airplay.

Burn your What? Alex Houston, one of the best ventriloquists in the business (his puppet's name was "Elmer") lived next door to us at the time. Years earlier, Alex had been on the *Jimmy Dean Show* out of Washington, DC. Dale knew him from there. I had a great idea, I thought. Why not record Alex and Elmer the puppet? We had to have a unique song. Mike Peavyhouse from Willex said, "Why don't you write one about burn your bra, baby?" That was when *burn your bra* was the popular thing to do. When Max D. Barnes and I were on one of the Willex shows and in our motel room, we got the guitars out and wrote "Burn Your Bra, Baby." I cut it on Alex and Elmer. I had a song for the B side, it was "Camp Chuga Chuga." I also produced a Christmas LP on Alex and Elmer called "Here Comes Peter Cotton Claus." Also included was one Dale and I wrote, "You Broke My Little Wooden Heart." It was weird. In the studio I found myself talking to Elmer the puppet more than to Alex!

Dale and I were on the road and had just finished an engagement. We were driving back to Nashville and stopped in Stuckey's to get a snack or two when over the speakers we heard a song that sounded familiar. I said, "Hey! That's my song!" It was "Love in the Hot Afternoon" by a new artist named Gene Watson. The song had been cut before by Jim Ed Brown on his *Evening* album - but it was just an album cut. We no more than got home when Vince Matthews called and said, "Rocker, we got us a hit!" It went to number two in the Billboard charts and won a BMI award in 1976. A short time later I got to meet Gene Watson. I was booked on a show in Palestine, Arkansas, with him. Boy! What a singer! Later, Gene sent me a *Best of Gene Watson* CD, which he had autographed - a very nice gesture.

I got a call one afternoon from Tommy Allsup, a record producer and lead guitar player. He said Clint Eastwood had just recorded "Love in the Hot Afternoon" and asked if I would like to come down and meet him. Gee, it don't get much better than that - Clint was one of my movie heroes! I went down to the studio and Clint was just finishing up. He came over and introduced himself. What a mild-mannered, soft-spoken guy he was, just like he is in the movies. He was six-four and I'm five-nine. You could say I kinda looked up to him. He said, "I sure like your song." However, the record company, Certron, he recorded it for went out of business and it never came out. I don't even have a copy of it.

It wasn't long after that when Waylon Jennings cut the same song for RCA. Ray Pennington produced it. Waylon had some throat problems that day and didn't like the way he came off on it, so it never got released - except on Bear Family Records sometime later. The Bear family was a German record company that bought or leased masters on artists that had been unreleased or older recordings, then re-released them on their label. Vickie Lawrence also recorded "Love in the Hot Afternoon," and it was a single on a private-stock label produced by Snuffy Garrett in California. In recent years, Mark Chestnutt had it on a CD.

At the time DeBeaux was dating Jimmy Jenkins, Conway Twitty's youngest son. Conway's real name was Harold Jenkins. Conway called me one night and wanted to come over and chat with me. Conway and I sat in the den and played songs and talked. He asked if it would be ok if he paid for DeBeaux's way through college. That was awfully nice of him. I said sure. As it turned out, she only went one semester and then dropped out. Conway produced Nat Stuckey on one of my tunes "The Shady Side Of Charlotte." It was a single.

Meanwhile back at Tootsie's, I was still hanging around. I remember Webb Pierce drove up in a customized car with chrome rifles on the sides, pistols for door handles, and bullhorns coming out of the grille, plus a real saddle for the interior with silver dollars all over the inside door panels and dash! He had to hire a guard to stand outside and watch the car while he went inside to drink beer.

Webb introduced us to his new manager, Roy Hall. Yes, you guessed it: Roy "The Hound" Hall. Roy was a rockabilly artist in the 1950s and recorded for Decca. He said he wrote "Whole Lotta Shakin' Goin' On" for Jerry Lee Lewis. Factually, it's a little unsure whether he really did or not. He might have, but Roy was always saying one thing and a moment later changing his story. At any rate, he didn't manage Webb for long. He still maintains that his recording of "Whole Lotta Shakin'" outsold Jerry Lee Lewis's version by millions. It didn't.

Around this time, Willex was starting to have some money problems, so they closed the record company and quit the music business.

Dale developed a thyroid problem, and she decided to quit the road. It was kinda lonesome out there without her. I can remember Dale had to have a minor operation. When she was in the hospital, I was coming up to see her one afternoon, and I suddenly fainted in the hall. They put me in the room next to her for a few minutes. She was fine, sitting up, reading a book and eating a sandwich. I was laid out.

About this time, Grant Grieves came to town from Kansas City with his wife, Marcia, and family. Grant was in the Rockabilly Hall of Fame for his Circle K records, "Shake It Baby," "Four on the Floor," and others. Grant was working with Pat McKinney with his two sons, Doug (he changed the spelling to "Dug") and Terry nicknamed "Toad." Dug was a great guitar player and Terry an excellent drummer. Pat had a few weeks off, so I hired Grant and the boys to go with me on some dates. Grant had a style like Jerry Lee Lewis. He and I became best friends. We both had grown up with the same backgrounds and tastes. We were riding in the car to a date one time, and we were just talking. I told Grant that when I was about eight years old, there was a song I had loved but now didn't know the words to, or even what the title was. I hummed the melody and - lo and behold - Grant sang the lyrics back to me! It was "Galavantin' Galveston

Gal," an obscure Gene Autry song. It was amazing. That reminded me of when we were kids and used to go to the theater on Saturdays when there would be two or three Western features, four or five cartoons, and a serial. Instead of candy or popcorn, I used to go to the drugstore before the movie and get a bottle of malt tablets. That's what I like for snacks. Still do. Grant said they were Horlick's malt tablets, and he did the same thing.

My Favorite Ant: We also had the same favorite movie actors, songs, and recording artists. Our lives paralleled each other in so many ways. I'll never forget one date we had, in New England, I think. We pulled up to the place where we were booked and the marquee sign said, "Now Playing: Kent Westberry and Ant Greves." The wind had blown off the *Gr* in front of *ant* and the *i* in Grieves. I said, "Ant Greves, huh? I wonder if *Uncle Greves* will be here too." For a long time after that we all called him "Ant Greves."

No Moose is Good Moose: One time we were booked into Newfoundland. We had to drive to Maine, take the ferry over to Nova Scotia, and drive the rest of the way. We rounded a curve, and there stood a giant moose, blocking the road. We honked the horn, but the moose didn't move. We just had to sit there till he left, about thirty minutes later. We were driving a Cadillac and pulling a trailer at the time. We got to the date site, and we had a two-week engagement there, I think. On the last night, it started snowing. Not ordinary snow - that was a *blizzard!* It was already over ankle-deep when we were packing up. Two older Canucks came by, started laughing, and said, "Lookathere," pointing to our car. "Summer tires. They'll never get out of Canada." We thought to ourselves "Oh! No!" But we did make it back. We were so sore from riding I traded the Cadillac for a new customized van and pulled a trailer from then on.

Back in Nashville, I had left Jack Music and was freelancing as a writer when I decided to give Mel Tillis a call. He had started his own publishing company, Sawgrass Music. Mel said "Wh..wh...what are y..you doing n..now?" I told him I was looking for a writing deal. He said come on over. I signed a writing deal with him. He put me on salary to pitch songs for the company too. One of my favorite artists from the 1950s was Tommy Collins. He was writing for Mel too. He had moved to Nashville from Bakersfield, California. Tommy had some hit songs in the fifties as an artist for Capitol Records: "You Better Not Do That," "Whatcha Gonna Do Now?" and "High on a Hilltop." Also, he wrote such hits as "Roots of My Raisin'" by Merle Haggard, "Carolyn" also by Merle, and lots of others.

I only stayed there about a year, then - as Willie would've sung - back on the road again. This time we were working with Jacky Ward and Reba McEntire. I opened the show, then my band backed them. We were out West some place - I can't remember exactly where (It's not *Alzheimer's* in my case - I call it *Oldtimer's Disease*). We did several shows together. Reba and Jacky were doing some duets at the time for Mercury Records. I don't think Reba had hit yet. Jacky had a hit with "Big Blue Diamonds." They were great to work with. I believe Jacky became pastor of a church later on.

Harlan Sanders and I started writing together a lot. Harlan referred to himself as "Handsome Harlan" Sanders. Harlan asked me if I'd produce a session with him. I said sure. He recorded "Them Booze Drinkin' Buddies of Mine" backed with "I Can Feel Him Touching You All Over Me." We wrote them both. They were released on Shannon Records, Mary Reeves' and the late Jim Reeves' company. Johnny Bush also recorded "I Can Feel Him Touching You." Harlan was a great guy. He was in prison earlier for quite a while for accidentally killing a man in a fight. Johnny Cash was instrumental in getting Harlan released from prison, as well as Glen Sherley, who wrote "Graystone Chapel" for Johnny.

Mary Reeves, Jim's widow, had Tuckahoe Music Publishing Company and wanted to sign Harlan to a writer's contract. Harlan told them he wanted me to be signed, too, as part of the deal. They agreed. So now we were writing for Tuckahoe Music. One of our first cuts over there was Eddy Arnold's "Love Me." That was followed by "I Finally Gave Her Enough Rope to Hang (And She's Still out there Swinging)" by Buck Owens.

Sounds Fishy to Me: One day Harlan decided he wanted to go fishing. He was living in some apartments off Walton Ferry Road in Hendersonville at the time. There was a lake in the back. He got a cane pole and some worms and threw his line in. Yep, he caught a little fish but couldn't reel him in with no reel. He put the cane pole on his shoulder, turned around, and started walking up the hill with the fish flapping on the other end. He got it up on land and hauled off and jerked it. The fish sailed up into the tree that was in the yard and wound around a limb. He just left it. So much for fishing! Harlan later co-wrote "If Drinking Don't Kill Me (Your Memory Will)" by George Jones.

Getting back to Grant Grieves. He wanted me to produce a session on him, so I did: "Good Time Girl" backed with "It's Times Like These" on Crackerbox Records. His sons Dug and Terry played on the session.

We got a call from Roy Hall who had started a booking agency, and he said he had us booked in Colorado. Dale went along as our girl singer. We drove all the way out there and pulled up to the club. The owner said, "We don't have you booked here. We already have a band." Boy, was I hot! I called Roy Hall and said, "What's going on? We're here in Colorado and they said we're not booked here!"

Roy said, "Oh my gosh! Let me get back to ya," and hung up. He *couldn't* call back – he hadn't even asked for our phone number! We were stuck, so we started driving back. Grant said, "I think I know someone in Kansas City where we can pick up a week. He made a call and got us a club date there for a week and saved the day. Needless to say, we didn't work for Roy anymore.

In the meantime, back at the Country Corner on Music Row where I spent a lot of afternoons, I met a guy named Billy Swan. Billy was the writer of the hit song "Lover Please" by Clyde McPhatter.

We used to hang around a little from time to time. He was a good writer. One afternoon he went into the studio and cut what was supposed to be the A side, but radio play flipped it over. The B side, "I Can Help," ended up being a monster hit!

Shortly after Kris Kristofferson moved to California, Billy followed and joined Kris's band. Kris had written the hit song "Me and Bobby McGee" for Janis Joplin and "Help me Make It Through the Night," by Sammi Smith, as well as "For the Good Times" by Ray Price - and many others. Kris was a helicopter pilot. One day in Nashville he landed a chopper right in Johnny Cash's back yard. He told the superstar he had a song for him. I guess Johnny figured anyone with the guts to land a helicopter in my yard, I'll take a few minutes to listen to what he has. Kris pitched him "Sunday Morning Comin' Down." Johnny had a big hit on it. Later Kris became a well-known movie personality.

At the time, Dale and I had been going to a Catholic church. Even though I was brought up Baptist, I had told the Lord I would go to His house on Sundays every time I could. We attended Our Lady of the Lake Church on Rockland Road in Hendersonville. I didn't understand the Latin part of the service, but we went just the same. Our group of about twenty-four people had started the church in a small school classroom. Father Arnold was the priest. Dale and I are considered members of the founding families. The church body kept growing, so we had to move several times to accommodate the increasing numbers. All our girls were musically involved in the church. For years we went there. Today, thousands of people worship at Our Lady of the Lake every Sunday.

Then one day someone told us about the Lord's Chapel, a nondenominational church that was on fire for the Lord in Brentwood, about thirty-five miles from us. We thought we'd try it. I had been praying for a church where both Dale and I could go to worship and feel completely at home. Billy Roy Moore was the pastor. We joined and we loved it. The Lord answered another prayer.

It seemed that everyone we knew was going there. Dale's good friend, Pat McKinney, was a member, as were many others: Grant and Marcia Grieves, Donna Stoneman of The Stonemans, Cathy Manzer, great singer and writer, Jeannie C. Riley, Maria and Alex Houston (Elmer the Puppet stayed home), and lots of other musicians we knew. Jeannie C. Riley, Dale, and I were baptized and rededicated our lives to the Lord on the same night.

Word from Above: A lot of amazing things happened at the Lord's Chapel. I remember once seeing what I can only describe as a whirlwind going down two rows of the church - and there were no doors opened! Also, I recall another time hearing the Lord ask from a voice inside me, "If you could have any gift you wanted in your life, what would it be?" I thought for a moment and said, "Happiness." I figured I'd have to have enough of everything else to be happy. It wasn't like I've ever been without. I've always been a happy person. Not that I don't have problems or sadness in my life – these happen to everyone. But I have managed to keep a positive, happy attitude through it all. I believe such optimism comes straight from God.

For quite a long time I had been a heavy smoker. I regularly smoked *three packs* of Kool cigarettes a day. I wanted to quit but couldn't. One day I prayed and asked the Lord if He would please remove the desire to smoke from me. After my prayer I walked to the dresser and laid a fresh pack of Kools on it. I have never smoked again – nor have I even *thought* of cigarettes again. Praise the Lord!

Dale did the *Ralph Emery Morning Show* every now and then. I even did it once. The only problem was we had to get up at four a.m. to get ready and drive to WSM Studios. Still, we enjoyed doing the show. Dale guested on the Grand Ole Opry several times, once on the Ernest Tubb portion. Ernest introduced her, and she sang "Are you from Dixie?" There had been no rehearsal, so the band didn't know where to come in! Being the trooper that she is, Dale sang both verses a cappella. The band finally came in on the chorus. The whole thing still sounded great.

Marijohn Wilkin, Kent, Tony Moon –
Buzz Cason showing our Beatles releases on the news.

Kent receiving BMI award for "Memory Maker." Left to right: Bill Denny, Mel Tillis, Dollie Denny – Kent. John Denny.

Freddy Weller on stage in Poland, Jay Shoupe on steel,
with my band the Memory Makers.

Dale Turner on the Midnight Jamboree –
Kent on guitar – Joe Edwards, fiddle.

Kent on stage in Poland – Jay Shoupe (steel)
Russ Kortright lead guitar. Mike Webb – bass.

Max D. Barnes, Elmer, Alex Houston

Kent: Receiving a BMI award for "Love in the Hot Afternoon." Jack Clement in white suit, far left Francis Preston, right: Roger Sovine.

Chapter 15

BRUSH IT ON, ROLL IT ON

I always painted our own houses and enjoyed doing it. I had painted rainbow swirls on the walls of our kid's bedrooms: purple, blue, orange, green, popsicle colors, and they loved it. One day a lady came over to the house and asked, "Who painted your house?" I said I did. She asked if I would paint her house. I went over and looked at it and gave her a bid. I painted her house, then a week or so went by, and I got a call from another lady who had seen the first lady's house and wanted me to paint hers. That's how I got into painting on the side.

Angel on the Housetop: At that time, I was gone two to three weeks at a time working clubs with a couple of weeks off in between to paint houses. During this time, I was painting an old three-story house on Music Row downtown. I had a forty-foot ladder stretched out all the way to reach the top part of the house and was dreading getting all the way up on top of the ladder. I asked the Lord to help me get enough courage to get up there. Halfway there, I heard a voice from below. It said, "You need some help?" I looked down and saw a young guy standing there. He said, "I'm a painter."

I said, "Sure, are you afraid of heights?" He said no and proceeded to climb up and paint all around the high places of the house.

97

I paid him and asked him if he could work the next day. He said yes. The next day he didn't show up. I called the number he gave me, but they said he was no longer there and they didn't know where he went. I believe to this day he was an angel. The Bible says we'll entertain angels. I'm not trying to preach, just trying to tell what happened.

Susan, our oldest daughter, was traveling with an all-girl band at this time. Susan was a great singer and songwriter. She also played bass, piano, and guitar. They had formed a band called Girl's Town. They even did a spot on Hee-Haw. Then they got a booking overseas to Holland. Susan took DeBeaux and Judy with her as singers. I don't remember how many weeks they were gone, but when they got back, Judy and DeBeaux said they'd had enough of the music business.

Susan went with me on quite a few shows playing bass and singing. We went to Jackpot, Nevada, with Kenny Price. It was cold and snowing. The shows went great, but there wasn't a lot to do there when you were off except play the slots - I think they design it that way. We got bored, so we built a snowman right up against the door of Kenny's motel room. He couldn't get out without knocking it down. We thought it was funny. He wasn't too amused.

By this time Judy and Susan had moved back into the house. De-Beaux had gotten married and moved out. Susan's friend, one of the girls from the all-girl band she worked with, moved in. It seemed like we always had one or two moving in and one or two moving out. Sometimes Susan, Gilda Jordan of the all-girl band, and Donna Atkinson would go out on the road with me. Susan would play bass, Gilda played piano, and Donna played lead guitar. They were all fine pickers and singers.

Let's Make a Deal: Smiley and Kitty Wilson were well-known Grand Ole Opry acts in an earlier time. Smiley had started his own booking agency. He was booking me and The Memory Makers band. At that time, he introduced me to Kirby Clifton, a builder in Goodlettsville. Kirby liked us and came to all the shows we did in the area. Kirby and I became friends. He had recently built several houses. One almost finished, and he said he wanted to show it to us. He added, "I'll give you guys a deal you can't refuse."

As we walked through the house, Dale said, "We could never afford this." It was a beautiful brick home with two levels, two fireplaces, a huge den, upstairs living room, big kitchen, dining room, and two-car garage. To our delight, Kirby did give us a price we couldn't refuse. I said, "We'll take it!"

The house sat on almost two acres. The back yard went straight up a hill. The grass was almost knee-deep, and all we had at the time was an old-fashioned push mower! I was out trying to mow the yard, and I guess the neighbors must've felt sorry for me, because they came from all sides with their riding lawnmowers - John on one side, Don Moore from the other side, and Bobby Borchers from up the hill in the back. More about Bobby later. Dale and I started praying for enough money to buy a riding mower. It wasn't a week or so later that a check came in the mailbox - for exactly to the penny what a new lawnmower cost. It wasn't a BMI check, it was from some radio performance company. I still don't know what it was for. I attribute this whole episode to tithing.

Clothes Make the Man: Bobby Borchers was a fine songwriter and singer. He had pretty good hits on "Whispers" and "Cheap Perfume and Candlelight" as an artist. He also wrote the song "Jamestown Ferry" with Mac Vickery for Tanya Tucker, among others. Bobby played the Western Room as a single between intermissions of the main shows. I always thought Bobby was a great talent. Bobby asked me to play a show with him using my band, The Memory Makers. I think it was a VFW club somewhere in Illinois. The motel we checked into was a little less than "ratty." The manager asked, "Do you know the guy that just checked in?" He must have known we were the band. Bobby's picture was up on the wall next to a fly swatter, behind the desk. The manager told us that Bobby had arrived in a limousine with a chauffeur who got out, opened the back door for him, and rolled out a red carpet. Then Bobby got out in a tuxedo and checked in.

That night at the club, Bobby came out in a white tuxedo with matching cape, holding a silver goblet. He asked if we could play "Jesus Christ, Superstar." With a four-piece band? Buddy Cannon, writer and record producer, was the bass player. Eddie Burton was the lead guitar player. We still talk about that.

Eddie and I became very close friends. He married Pat McKinney after she and Dick Flood split up. Not only was Eddie a great guitar player (he played a lot of sessions in Nashville), he also wrote a lot of great songs. One such hit song that Eddie wrote was "Dancing your Memory Away" with Tom Grant, recorded by Charley McClain. He also had songs cut by Conway Twitty, George Jones, Tammy Wynette, and others. He also recorded a gospel album on his own.

At this time Susan was on the road with Barbara Allen in another all-girl band. Judy had moved out. I was booked in Alaska. Jimmy Case had booked me in Fairbanks at a club. We flew from Nashville to Fairbanks, the farthest point before the North Pole. Most of the day was night, and it was cold. After the first week we got paid by check, I sent the check home for Dale to put in the bank. After the second week, the check had bounced. I was madder than a wet hen. I went to the club manager and told him. He said he was sorry and wrote me another one.

And Bounce Some More: In the meantime, I had contacted the air base in Fairbanks, and they asked us to play there on Sunday night. We were off on Sunday night from the club. After the first Sunday at the air base they hired us for the second Sunday. I called Dale, and she said the *second* check from the club had bounced. I went to the manager again and demanded to know what was going on. He assured me that he had some money coming in the next week from Anchorage and it would cover everything. I had my doubts.

At the end of the third week *another* check had bounced. Prior to all this, he had also hired Little David Wilkins and his band to play the club opposite us. Little David had the hit single "Butter Beans" and wrote "Coming on Strong" for Brenda Lee, and many others. I told Little David what was going on, and he was a little nervous also. Little David, his band, and mine had a pretty good time together despite all the problems. Come to find out the manager was a member of a biker gang in Fairbanks. I finally went to him and said, "The band and I aren't going to play anymore. Why don't we just terminate the contract? Just fly us home and we'll forget it." I might add here that you couldn't drive out of Fairbanks if you wanted to. The only road out was a "trail" through solid ice and snow.

Bouncing Right into the Air: He finally agreed and wrote us a check for the flight. The band and I went to the airport. They loaded all our equipment on the plane, but then the guy behind the ticket counter said, "I can't accept this check. It's no good." He said, "I sold the club you were playing in to that guy, and I know his check is no good." The plane was on the runway and fixing to take off.

I told the man behind the counter, "All our clothes and everything we have are on that plane. We've got to get on it!"

He said, "Oh, all right, I'll deal with the guy at the club later. Hurry up and get on." We all ran out, boarded the plane, and took off for home. Every now and then I hear from Little David and he says, "Let's go back to Alaska." We both laugh. By the way, thanks to the air force base in Fairbanks for saving our hides!

And it Shall be Given unto You: It was about here I decided I wanted to come out of the clubs and start working one-nighters, being the opening act for other artists. My band would back the other artists. The only drawback was I didn't have the sound equipment that would carry far enough in auditoriums. I only had two Vocal Master columns with four smaller speakers in each one. It was okay for clubs and small venues but not for concerts. I didn't have thousands of dollars to put out for one. Dale and I prayed again. The Lord says in His word if you have a need, just ask in Jesus' name and you shall receive it. Well, I had met a guy named Bob at a party a year or so earlier. He called me out of the clear blue sky. I had met him only once. He asked if I would like to have all the Black Diamond guitar strings I could use.

Of course I would! I asked him, "You don't by any chance have a PA set, do you?"

He said, "We do. We have our first PA set and equipment coming off the line now. Do you need one?" YES! It was a *Ross system!* He said, "You might need to endorse for it." I said I would!

Lee Greenwood was also given one of these. Ray Pillow first introduced me to Lee at Pete Drake's recording studio. Lee was singing at the piano, and he had just come to town. Ray said, "What do you think of the song Lee's singing?" I said it sounded like a hit to me. It was.

Here Comes Santa Claus: About a week later, a tractor-trailer backed into my driveway and started unloading. Now I had two fifteen-inch Ross speaker columns with horns, two floor monitors, a twenty-four channel stereo mixing board, another mixing board for monitors, and two separate amps. Wait, there's more: two monitor hot spots, seven microphone stands and microphones, two electric solid body guitars, crates of guitar strings. I used my last set forty years later. It was like Christmas!

Getting Right with the Lord: Dale and I were riding over to Hendersonville, a suburb on the north side of Nashville, when the Lord spoke to me and said, "If you don't straighten up and change your lifestyle, you're not going to have Dale for long - I'll take my blessing back!" That scared me. I turned to her and told her, "Honey, as of now I quit drinking and taking pills and everything. I'm a new man." I pretty much was. I have fallen off the wagon a few times, but not many.

The Buddy Lee Agency started booking me and the band. We were working with The Wilburn Brothers, Teddy and Doyle, on a lot of fair dates, as well as Charlie Walker, Ray Pillow, Billy Grammar, Nat Stuckey, Lorrie Morgan, Roni Stoneman, Mary Lou Turner, with a few dates with Charlie Daniels. We also played a lot of shows with Peggy Sue, Loretta Lynn's sister, and her husband, Sonny Wright, as well as Charlie Louvin. We were sitting in the car behind the stage at one show, and I told Charlie about a song Eddie Burton and I had written. It was "Drink It Over." I had a tape with me and played it. Charlie said, "I'll do it." He did.

We got a call from another booking agency that had put together a string of one-nighters (thirty-one in all) at Freightliners Truckstops of America outlets. It was called the *Charlie Douglas Road Show* starring Dave Dudley, who had the hit "Six Days on the Road." The group included Becky Hobbs, David Rogers, Delilah McClain, and me and my band. We worked all through the South and Midwest.

Whispers from the Past: Dale went with us on most of the trips. And she would go with me on most of the other dates we had. I loved history, and we'd stop everywhere we could, like when we were in San Antonio, we visited the Alamo. When we were in South Dakota, we went by Mount Moriah and visited Wild Bill Hickock's (James Butler Hickock) grave. Right next to his was Calamity Jane's grave (Martha Jane Canary). We visited the Custer battlefield where Custer's Last Stand took place at Little Big Horn in Montana. When we were in Virginia, we went to the Natural Bridge. Underneath the bridge was a rock wall where George Washington signed his name, along with Thomas Jefferson. We visited Mount Rushmore where the presidents' heads are carved in rock. We also played St. Joseph, Missouri, at an old movie theater and saw the old Jessie James house, where Bob Ford killed Jessie. Another one of my heroes was Davy Crockett. When Dale and I went to Gatlinburg for a vacation, we continued on to Greensboro to see Davy's birthplace and home. There's a monument there and an old log cabin right next to a creek like the one he was born in. The original had burned down years ago. The feeling was still there. So many places to see in America!

Back in Nashville I did a session for Doorknob Records. Gene Kennedy was the producer. I recorded "Easy Lady" and "If the Whole World was an Ashtray," as well as "She Gets to Me" and "Tinseltown." The latter was never released. All these were original songs. Gene was one of the best producers around. He also produced for

Peggy Sue, Loretta Lynn's sister, and Sonny Wright as well as Wayne Kemp, Bobby G. Rice, and others for the label.

During this time, The Memory Makers and I were playing the Nashville Palace out by Opryland. Lib Hatcher was manager of the Palace. She also managed Randy Travis, a new artist she was trying to promote. Randy Traywick was his real name. He had cut two records for Paula Records earlier. For a short while they changed his name to Randy Ray, but later decided on Randy Travis. Randy was working at the Palace as a cook in the kitchen, and he would get up with us on occasion and sing. We worked there off and on for about a year. Of course, Randy went on to become one of country music's biggest stars.

Word from Above: The Lord spoke to me again one night while I was saying my prayers. I always mention to Him that He comes first in my life, above all things. While I was saying this, I was interrupted by a voice somewhere inside that said, "No, you don't." It stopped me in my tracks. I knew it was the Lord talking. I said, "What do you mean, Lord?"

He said, "What's the first thing you do in the morning?"

"I get my coffee and get on my computer."

He replied, "See"?

I was astounded. "Oh, I never thought of that." He wanted me to put Him first by reading a chapter of His Word in the Bible and saying a prayer every day. I've done that ever since, as well as adopting the verse, "Today's a day the Lord has made. I will rejoice and be glad in it."

Around this time Pat McKinney and Eddie Burton were married. Eddie asked me to be best man. Eddie played lead guitar for Pat on a lot of her shows. Later he worked with me too. Eddie had worked with Jacky Ward for a while before joining the group "The In." Eddie and I wrote Buck Owens' last single "Forever Yours" before Buck passed away.

Dale and I were on the road again. After the show we were in the motel room when I got a call from Dave Burgess from Nashville with Republic Records and Lariat Music Publishing Co., which he owned.

Dave also said he had recorded one of my songs with Bobby G. Rice for Republic. It was "The Softest Touch in Town." As soon as I got back to Nashville I went to see Dave and signed with him.

Dave and I wrote several songs for Bill Nash on the Republic label, including "Saturday Night Live" and "Fingertip Fever." David Rogers was also on that label and recorded two of my songs, "Farewell to Arms" and "The Lady's All Dressed Up for Love." Tom Grant also recorded one of David Rogers' and my songs, "We've Got To Get Away From It All." The Champs (who had "Tequila") were going to do a new album called *Tejano Nights*, a CD. Dave and I wrote a song for it, an instrumental titled "Frijoles."

I started writing some gospel songs and wrote one with Max D. Barnes and Hal Harbour called "See That Light on Yonder Mountain." The Chuck Wagon Gang recorded it, as well as The Greenes.

I was on a lot of package shows with Charlie Walker and Ray Pillow. During that time, I did a song I'd written called "One Too Many Memories." Ray asked me later if he could record that one. I said sure, and Ray recorded it. In the studio at the time was Mel Tillis. Ray asked Mel to sing the harmony part and Mel did, even though he didn't get credit on the record.

I was also doing a lot of shows with Ferlin Husky and his alter ego, "Simon Crum." Ferlin and Simon would get into arguments with each other. That was hilarious. We also worked with Sheb Wooley, the actor-singer-songwriter. Sheb wrote "Purple People Eater," as well as many other hits. He also had a comedy side named "Ben Colder."

My mom and dad would come up and visit us from time to time. I remember one time I took my dad downtown to Music Row to show him around, and we stopped in at Dave Burgess's office. Chet Atkins was there with Dave. Dave said, "Come on in." We went in, and I introduced Dad to Dave and Chet. They all shook hands. Later when we got outside, Dad said, "Who was that? Chet Atkins, the guitar man?" I said YES! Dad turned to me and said, "Holy mackerel, I just shook Chet Atkins' hand!"

This one Quacked 'em Up: Back on the road again, I had a new bass player who was always grouchy. We were on our way to play a show someplace. The band and I were all in the van riding down the road, and it was hot. The air was on but way in the back you couldn't feel it very well. The bass player woke up, growled, and complained, "You need to run some ducts back here."

I said, "We did, and they pooped all over the place so we had to chase them off!" Everyone broke up and we laughed for thirty miles.

Was this Trip Really Necessary? One time, Mel Tillis was on the show, and the announcer said, "Ladies and gentlemen, let's welcome Mel Tillis!" Mel came running out and tripped on the microphone cord. The microphone rocked forward, then swung back and hit Mel smack in the mouth. Mel said *"Sssshit!"* right over the mic.

Keep your Fiddle to Yourself: Another funny story was that Hank Snow was on the Opry one night, and Chubby Wise was playing fiddle for him. In the middle of "I'm Movin' On," Chubby stepped up to the mic, playing his part, and the fiddle bow took off Hank's toupee. Hank turned to Chubby and said, "Chubby, you're fired!"

I ran into Billy Walker one afternoon on Music Row and Billy said, "Why don't you and I write some songs for an upcoming album I'm going to do?" It was a Western album, all cowboy songs. I said okay and told him I had an idea for a Western song anyway. It was "Buenos Noches Nacogdoches." We got together and wrote it and nine other songs out of the twelve that were on the LP. It came out on Tall Texan Records, Billy's label. The title song was "Wild Texas Rose."

After about a year or so writing for Dave Burgess I was freelancing again. I started my own publishing company, Memory Maker Music. That way, I could keep writing for someone else or write for my own company. I worked Florida a lot during this period with the band. On one such occasion I was working a club date, and Dale was with me. An old girlfriend from the past was in the audience with her mother, and she asked if I'd like to see a picture of my daughter. She showed me the girl's picture and said her name was Dawn. She looked to be in her late twenties. It took me by surprise, to say the least! I remember that I had thought she might be pregnant when we split up. More about this later.

I first met Buzz Cason when Snuffy and I first came to Nashville. Buzz was working with The Casuals who were backing Brenda Lee at the time. The Casuals had several good records out on their own. Buzz was also with The Crickets, Buddy Holly's band after Holly's death. Buzz had the hit record *Look for A Star* under the name Gary Miles. I ran into Buzz one afternoon and told him I was looking for a writing deal. Buzz said he needed a "meat-and-potatoes" writer for his company, meaning a writer who can write all styles of music. I went to work with him. Gene Watson recorded one of our songs, "The Winds of Change (are Blowing me Away)." Buzz also wrote several hits himself: "Everlasting Love" by Gloria Estefan and "Soldier of Love," co-written with Tony Moon and recorded by Arthur Alexander – and The Beatles - and many others

Still working the road, I was booked on a show with Freddy Weller. For those who don't know, Freddy was the lead guitar player for Paul Revere and The Raiders rock group. Freddy went out on his own and recorded "Games People Play." It was a monster hit written by Joe South. Freddy was a great showman, singer, and writer. Freddy also wrote "Lonely Women Make Good Lovers," a hit for Bob Luman, and the hit "Dizzy" by Tommy Roe and others. One night after the show he said, "Why don't we write one together?" So we did. Freddy was from Atlanta. We did quite a few shows together. I loved working with him, and we started writing a lot together. It wasn't long before Freddy and his wife, Pippy, moved to Brentwood, a suburb of Nashville.

Guess They all can't be Peaches and Cream: Then we got booked on a Marlboro tour to Poland – Freddy, my band, The Memory Makers, and me. We went to Warsaw. They were still under Russian rule. I remember we checked into the hotel and the guy that brought in the bags whispered to us, "Don't say anything negative about the government or the people in charge. The rooms are bugged." We had a designated bus and driver who drove us around, to and from the places we played. The food was awful. The fruits and vegetables were in carts on the sidewalks and most of them were borderline rotten. In the hotel restaurant the smell was terrible. It smelled like spoiled food. I couldn't eat most of it. We ate a lot of peanut butter. The city square was nice. Artists would paint their pictures there and sell them. I bought one. Horse-drawn carriages would take you down the old brick roads on a tour of the old city. You could hardly drink the Polish beer, but the Czech beer and the German beer weren't bad. They said you can't drink the water. On one occasion I did - and got dysentery!

The first thing Freddy and I did when we hit the U.S. and got off the plane was to make a beeline for the first hot dog stand we could find!

I hadn't been back long before I had a call asking if I wanted to play a show on a cruise to the Bahamas featuring Moe Bandy, Johnny Lee, Tom Bresh, Lane Brody, and others. I did, and I got to take Dale on that one. Bill Bowers (Bowermaster) was Darrell McCall's cousin and was playing bass with Moe. Moe's band backed me. These were good times.

Then the band and I were booked at Gilley's Rodeo Arena in Texas with Darrell McCall, Diane McCall, Johnny Bush, and others. After that they had the Music Valley Festival, right down the street from the Nashville Palace where I still occasionally still played. They had a tent set up and had built a big stage. The band and I opened the show. It was an all-day event. We backed a lot of artists: Johnny Rodriguez, Lorrie Morgan, Freddy Weller, and Ray Pillow, just to name a few.

Normally on my shows I do a Grand Ole Opry segment. In the middle of it I do impersonations of a lot of artists, including Ernest Tubb, Hank Snow, Marty Robbins, Roy Acuff, and Johnny Cash. At one show I noticed Roy Acuff and "Bashful Brother" Oswald sitting in the front row. I omitted the Roy Acuff part from my impersonations.

I figured however well I did it, I couldn't do him justice, so I left it out. When the show was over, Roy Acuff came up to me and said, "Son, I believe you do the best Johnny Cash I ever heard." What a nice compliment.

My daughters: Judy and DeBeaux

My daughter – Dawn.

My daughters, L to R – Susan Thomsen Clark,
and DeBeaux, Judy McClure in center.

My daughter, Susan Thomsen Clark and Kent back stage.

My darling wife Dale, and me.

Kent – Gary Hart on bass –Eddie Burton
on lead guitar at the Villages in Florida

Chapter 16

ON THE HOME FRONT

One night I was downtown and I fell off the wagon. I had a couple of beers. Someone gave me a Benzedrine pill, and I took it. The next morning, I woke up and I couldn't move my face on one side. I looked like a pirate. I could only smile a half a smile and couldn't close one eye. I had Bell's palsy. I went to the hospital. They wanted to operate right then, but Dale said, "No." We left and went to an ear, nose, and throat specialist. He gave me some electric shocks in my face. He also gave me some pills to take that burned like fire under my skin. Dale and I prayed hard. About three weeks later, I woke up one morning and it was gone. Just like that. I never made that mistake again!

I was still painting houses. I got all the work I wanted from a little ad I ran in the local bargain paper. At times I would even have to take the ad out because I was so busy. Mel Tillis had bought Cedarwood Publishing and shortly after sold it to BMG, a conglomerate. In the meantime, Dale and I started looking for another house. I found one I fell in love with. It was pretty rough and needed a lot of work, but I could see how it would look when it was finished. Dale always let me have my way. She always said God made me the head of the house.

This Big Ol' House: It was a large home: three thousand square feet on three acres with plenty of beautiful trees. It looked like a park. The house was shaped like a barn, with the front door recessed into the roof. They called it a *Mansford* roof. It had five wooden steps going up to the door. The inside had the old, 1950s wavy ceramic sink in the kitchen and no cabinets, just a freestanding pantry. No central heat or air and none of the doors would lock. It was a two-story with three big glass windows in the den and strips of mustard yellow, pink, and blue carpet in the living room. I had to have it. I knew I could fix it up. Besides, we had plenty of money from the profit of selling the other one. A day or two after we moved in, it started pouring rain and the dirt driveway turned into mud. Dale drove up with two of her girlfriends to show them the house and they got a few mud splatters on them. They all sat out on the porch and cried and commiserated.

I started right in fixing it up. I even replaced all the thresholds, realigned all the doors, added central heat and air, and installed new kitchen cabinets. I built indirect lighting in the kitchen and put in new carpets. In short, I completely renovated the house. I gave it new paint inside and out, built a front half-circle deck, and added three A-frames on the front, one over the front door and two more A-frames over the two recessed windows. It looked great! It took me two years, but it was worth it. I found a big oak tree stump and an old wagon wheel, then mounted the wheel on the stump and got glass cut to fit on the wheel. It made the neatest Western-style coffee table for my writing room. Dale finally started liking the house.

We were only blocks from the church we were going to. The first Sunday we went, we saw Doug Jernigan. Doug and I had worked together a few times. He was considered one of the best steel guitar players in Nashville. There was Ron Stroup, a drummer who also worked with Dale and me when he first came to Nashville, and good friend Bill Rippy on lead guitar, who worked with Faron Young and others. It was like Old Home Week. Donnie and Vickie Clark were good songwriters and singers as well. They also played in the church band. Donnie and I had something in common: he also painted houses on the side. He and I painted together on the same jobs from time to time. More about him later.

Judy had gotten married a year after DeBeaux and later had a daughter she named Coty Lyn. I became a grandpaw for the first time.

Me and The Boys from Britain: I was on the road again, and one of my band members told me he loved my song "I Just Don't Understand" and that he especially liked The Beatles version. I told him he was wrong, that The Beatles had never recorded it. He said, "Yes, they did! I've got the cassette tape on it by them." Sure enough, it was on a bootleg album. *Well, shoot your mama and call me Sally if it wasn't true - I had a Beatles song!*

Then a few weeks later, an article came out in the *Tennessean* newspaper saying that The Beatles, before they hit big, used to go over to a local radio station of the BBC in England and jam after they got through with their club dates. They were getting ready to release some of those songs. My song was one of them. It came out on Capitol Records, *Live at the BBC,* LP and CD. It eventually sold around two million copies. Neither the publishing company nor Marijohn Wilkin, the other writer, even knew about it.

Marijohn and I were downtown on Music Row doing a news interview about the song when Chet Atkins came over and said, "I produced that song." We thanked Chet for doing so. Tony Moon, lead guitar player earlier with The Casuals and Buzz Cason, also had a Beatles cut, "Soldier of Fortune," that came out on the same CD. Just thought I'd mention here that Marijohn Wilkin's son was John Bucky Wilkin who was the Ronny of Ronny and The Daytonas, a surf rock group.

Ben Hall had a recording studio off Dickerson Road out by Starday Records. I cut a lot of demos there as well as a couple of masters. I liked Ben. He was a great engineer and easy to work with. Ben was a good friend of Buddy Holly's and was a disc jockey in Lubbock, Texas, Buddy's hometown. Back when Buddy first started out and was recording for Decca, he cut one of Ben's songs: "Blue Days, Black Nights." Ben also had a country band at that time, and Buddy worked with him some.

Buddy was one of my favorite artists. Ben told me he had some of Buddy's old guitars and some tapes of recorded material Buddy had done back then that were never released. WOW!!! I had gone out there to see Ben one afternoon for something - I don't remember what - and there was a guy at the microphone just finishing up a vocal on some demos. Ben said, "Wait around a few minutes and I'll be done. Besides, I want you to meet the next country superstar." I said okay. When the guy finished he came into the control booth. Ben said "Kent, meet Garth Brooks."

We shook hands and I said, "Sure like your singin'."

He grinned and said, "Thanks, man." Ben was right. It wasn't long after that Garth had his first hit.

One afternoon I got a phone call. The voice on the other end said, "This is Dawn, your daughter," from the prior relationship I mentioned earlier in the book. She said she'd like to meet me and get to know me if it was okay. She wanted to come up. I said sure. I told Dale, and she thought that was a good idea. It wasn't long before Dawn and her husband and daughter came up to visit. We accepted her as one of the family. She had two other sons we got to meet later on. Suddenly, I was a grandpaw again.

A little later DeBeaux had a daughter named Brittany. That makes five grandkids. I was getting old before my time.

I was working the Nashville Palace again. Pee Wee King was our guest, and my band backed him up. He was such a nice man. He had written so many songs: "Bonaparte's Retreat," "You Belong to Me," "Tennessee Waltz," and "Slowpoke," a big pop hit in the 1950s. That's just to name a few, all written with Redd Stewart.

It was around this time Jerry Reed did "I Just Don't Understand" for his *Hot a'Mighty* album. A rock group called Spoon had just come out with the song, and it was also in the movie *Legion* with Dennis Quaid.

Melba Montgomery and I were writing some together. She recorded one we wrote called "Goin' Quietly Crazy." Johnny Duncan recorded another one of ours, "Watching Elizabeth Play."

I was painting a house one day, and the lady I was working for had the TV on. I saw one of the Twin Towers get hit. A few seconds later the other one got hit. I called Dale and told her to turn on the TV. It was a dark day: 9/11/2001.

Wayne Gray and I kept in touch by phone. He had gotten married again and was living in Mississippi. He was a DJ on a local radio station there. Wayne had invented the "Git Fiddle" as he called it. He would play his guitar with a fiddle bow. He got very proficient at it, especially with "Orange Blossom Special." Snuffy was also married again and owned a spa and tanning salon in Donelson, Tennessee.

I always felt I was so blessed to be able to make a good living doing something that I loved to do, but now I thought would be a good time to retire from the music business. I threw all my publicity material away - pictures, bios, etc. - and didn't pick up my guitar for a little over a year. I would, however, play at church occasionally. I told the Lord a long time ago that if I got asked to sing or play for Him, I wouldn't say no. I still do that.

Chapter 17

RECORDS, PATSY CLINE, AND UNCLE REMUS

I have always collected records and have accumulated quite a large number of them. One day I was in Hendersonville at one of the thrift stores looking for records when Donnie Clark came up. We talked, and I told him I had retired. He said, "I don't live but a few blocks away. How about coming by and seeing my recording studios?" Well…I said okay and went to his house. He had a nice little studio. He said, "I got this song I'm stuck on." He asked me to help him with it. It was called "I'm not Perfect, Just Forgiven," a gospel song. The whole last verse just popped into my head. From then on, I started writing again. Throughout the years, I've had a lot of people ask how I write a song. I've always remembered what Hank Williams once said: "I just hold the pen, and God writes them for me." That's about it. I always hear a linc (a *hook line* as they call it) come into my head, usually with the melody already. Sometimes it's quick, sometimes it's slow.

I got a call from Jerry Rivers who had played fiddle for Hank Williams and was booking talent for Buddy Lee's agency. He asked if I could get a band together and be the musical director for the *Patsy*

Cline Always Show, on the road. They were playing the old Ryman Auditorium. It was starring a young girl, Mandy Barnett, and another girl, just the two of them. It was a musical play about Patsy and a girl-friend. They wanted to take the "play" on the road. The house band they had at the Ryman didn't want to go out of town. I thought about it for every bit of ten seconds and said, "Yeah, I'll do it." I had never done this kind of thing before. It wasn't like a concert where you just get up and sing, it was more like a Broadway type show. Everyone had to read charts and play exactly what's written so the two actor/singers would know where to come in with their dialogue and songs. I got a great band put together, and we traveled for over a year doing those shows to sell-out crowds. The money was great, and all expenses were taken care of. Dale went with me on some of the shows.

Winds of Change: A funny thing happened one night during a performance. We were right in the middle of one of Patsy's songs when someone opened the backstage door and a gust of wind blew all the charts off the music stand of our bass player, Ric Boyer. Sheet music went flying everywhere! We all busted out laughing. It's a good thing Ric was such a good player and knew all of Patsy's songs anyway. He had to play the rest of the show by ear.

Some very close friends of ours, Lester and Carol Wilson, used to ride up to some of the shows and run around with Dale and me. We always had a good time together. I first met them at a record show in Nashville where I used to set up and sell records. Lester was a record collector and musician too. They would come by my booth and chat. They were from Connecticut. I just had to mention them.

Glenn Sutton also used to set up at the record shows. He, too, was a fine writer, with songs like "Almost Persuaded," "I Don't Wanna Play House" by Tammy Wynette, and "What Made Milwaukee Famous," as well as many others. He married Lynn Anderson.

Keep this One Under your Hat: I heard a story on how the song "Blue Bayou" was written. I don't know how true it is. It goes like this: Roy Orbison and Joe Melson were riding along in their convertible in New Orleans one afternoon and were stopped at a traffic light. An ample, well-dressed lady was crossing the street wearing a big hat. A gust of wind came up and took that hat and sailed it right past their windshield. Joe turned to Roy and said, "Did you see what just blew by you"? Roy said what a great idea for a song - *Blue Bayou*.

Down the Bunny Trail: Susan had moved to Jacksonville, Florida, and Dawn was living in Ft. Myers, Florida. Dale and I decided to go down and visit them. I need to mention here that one of my all-time favorite movies was *Song of the South* with Uncle Remus and Brer Rabbit and Brer Bear. Dawn had told me that on her way home another time she found the historical cabin and museum where it all began. I couldn't believe it. I had to go! On the way to Jacksonville to see Susan we stopped in Eatonton, Georgia. At the time there was nothing there but a gas station, a motel, a small grocery store, and a streetlight – and the museum was in an old cabin. All the other slave cabins are gone, but the feeling is still there. Inside was a collection of stories that young Joel Chandler Harris had heard from the slaves and had written in books revolving around Uncle Remus. In front of the cabin is a marker of Brer Rabbit standing against a historical marker. Dale couldn't get over the fact I had driven forty miles out of the way to see a plastic rabbit.

I ran into Dallas Frazier again. He was pastoring his own church right down the street from where we lived. We went several times to see him. Dallas was a very good preacher, but we felt obligated to attend our own church too. We also attended a Bible study that he had several times.

Well, I'll be Doggone! I remember another incident that occurred on the road. Dale, me, and the band were driving along on the interstate, pulling a trailer. We saw a fellow with a dog hitchhiking on the side of the road. We went on by. About thirty minutes later we saw the same guy with the dog on the side of the road again. He had gotten ahead of us somehow. We went on by the second time. About forty-five minutes later, there was the same man with the same dog standing on the side of the road, hitchhiking. Charlie, my drummer, was driving. He said, "I'm gonna stop and pick him up. I can't pass him again." We picked him and the dog up and put them in the front seat of the van. We were all just small-talking when suddenly sirens went off in all directions. Cop cars on all sides motioned us to pull over. One cop walked up to the driver's side and told Charlie to put his hands on the steering wheel. He complied and asked the cops what was going on. We explained who we were - that we were a band and had just picked this guy up to give him and the dog a ride. The cops said the guy was wanted for grand theft auto! They took him and the dog off and let us go on our way.

It seemed like we were working Florida a lot these days. Quite a few of the shows were with The Jordanaires, who backed Elvis. We opened the show for them and backed them up on several occasions.

Jerry Cooper was a new artist who had recorded several songs by Eddie Burton and me. He had a booking in Atlantic City at the Claridge Hotel and wanted Eddie, me and the band to do the shows with him. We did. That was a lot of fun. The boys and I went up to Atlantic City and got checked into the hotel. Jerry, his wife, Babs, and my wife came up in a limousine a day later. I hit the slot machine for $175, but the hotel got it all back.

During one of our shows Al Martino, the famous pop singer, came in to see us. Al was sitting at a table when the MC jumped up on stage and announced, "Ladies and gentlemen, we have a special guest with us tonight in the audience - Al *Martinez!*" We all felt like crawling under the stage.

Mel Tillis had started a new publishing company, Tillis Tunes. He had sold his other companies, Sawgrass Music and Cedarwood, to BMG, who in turn sold them again. At any rate, they all ended up with Universal Music Publishing Group. I gave him a call and he said, "I could use you as a writer over here." So I went back with Mel. He also had acquired Pete Drake's old recording studio, and we did most of our demos there. Curt Ryle was one of Mel's writers - and a great singer, I might add. He and I wrote several songs there. Mel Tillis Jr. (they called him "Sonny Boy"), another great singer and writer, was also on the roster.

I stayed with Mel about a year and was getting restless. I didn't care a whole lot about the newer country music they were playing. Everything was getting rock orientated. Radio wasn't playing the old style of country as I knew it. I decided to retire again. I was doing well enough financially, so I didn't have to do what I didn't want to do. But the music business is a hard thing to quit. I kept getting pulled back into it.

We had moved my mom and dad up from Florida a year earlier. They had a house not far from where we were. Dad never really liked it. He was a dyed-in-the-wool Floridian. He had Alzheimer's and wasn't getting any better. Mama always wanted to go back to Florida too. Within a year my dad passed away. We sold Mama's house and moved her to a nice apartment in an assisted living place right down the street where we could keep an eye on her.

*A House is Not...:.*Brad and Norma Burton were very close friends we had met at church. We started running around together. They were in real estate and owned a lot of property. They had a place in Lakeland, Florida, where they would go and spend winters. On one of these occasions, Dale and I decided to go down and visit with them for a couple of weeks. One afternoon we were all out driving around and ran into a new subdivision they were building. You could pick out your own lot and have a house built on it. Brad said, "If you buy one, I'll buy one next door to you." It sounded good to me, so I picked out a lot that had three big trees on it so I could put a hammock between two of them. Brad picked the one next to it. They said it would take about six months to build our houses. We picked out everything we wanted in ours. We decided to downsize from the 3,000-square-foot home in Nashville to a 2,160-square-foot home in Lakeland. Lakeland is halfway between Tampa and Orlando. We went back home and put our house up for sale.

In the meantime, DeBeaux was divorced and Susan was married to Ray Mosier and living in Jacksonville, Florida. They had formed a little band and were working locally. Judy was married to Gary McClure, a distant relative of the famous World War I hero, Sergeant York, and living in Nashville.

We got a call from Lakeland saying our house was ready. Norma and Brad had been overseeing it and keeping us posted on how it was doing. Norma, still in real estate, was selling our house in Tennessee too. We said goodbye to the house on Lee Road in Tennessee. We rented a U-Haul truck. The first load was one mattress and a chair, and all the rest were my records. A whole truck full! Dale said, "Why couldn't you have collected stamps?"

The Lakeland house was beautiful, just what we wanted. Norma and Brad had owned a mobile home real close to our new one, and we bought it from them for my mom. We moved my mom down with Shiloh, our dog. After several trips back and forth we finally made it. It seems like right after the last trip Norma sold our house in Tennessee.

A very short time later, Eddie Burton and Pat McKinney Burton moved down to Lakeland too, about ten minutes away from us. Eddie moved down first and stayed with us till he could get a job. He found one at the Regional Medical Center as a security guard. Then Pat moved down. I was still painting houses and enjoying it. Eddie said, "Why don't we play some of the RV parks down here"? I thought, "That's a good idea." I made some phone calls and landed a few jobs. It was fun. Then we branched out, got a little band together, and started working on some other venues.

Merv Shiner had moved to Tampa, which was only an hour away. I would go visit him. Tony Moon - who I mentioned earlier in this book - moved down to Sarasota. I stay in touch with him. George Hamilton IV would come down and play some of these parks, and we would go see him. George was doing a gospel album for Heart of Texas records in Brady, Texas. In that album he recorded one of my gospel songs, "The Love and Not the Nails."

Light at the End of the Funnel? "Funnel of Love" (that I mentioned earlier in this book, written in the early 1960s with Charlie McCoy, and recorded by Wanda Jackson) had just come out by Terraplane Sun, a rock group from California, and had also been played in several movies. The first movie was *But I'm A Cheerleader*. Then came *Rock N Rolla*, *Playing for Keeps* with Catherine Zeta-Jones and Gerard Butler, *Three Brothers and A Bride* with David Arquette, and yet another movie with Tilda Swinton called *Only Lovers Left Alive*. They also used it for a Nexium commercial in England and in the TV series *NCIS New Orleans*. Wanda Jackson re-recorded it under the direction of Jack White, a well-known rock producer. Wanda said she had to re-learn the song because she had so many requests for it. Not bad for a B side!

Tony Booth, who had previous hits on "Cinderella" and "Lonesome 7-7203" also recorded for Heart of Texas records and recorded several of Eddie Burton's and my songs. He did "Forever Yours," "Losing You Just Dawned on Me Today," "The Bridge to Memory Lane," and others. Darrell McCall also recorded for the label and did "Hello Out There."

Alex Houston, his wife, Sherry - and Elmer, of course - had a mobile home in Zephyrhills, about fifteen minutes from Lakeland. They would come down and stay the winter in Florida. We played some more shows with him. I always loved working with Alex and Elmer.

Then I got word that Snuffy in Nashville wasn't doing well, and they were doing a benefit for him in Cookeville, Tennessee. They asked if I could do it. Of course I could! Dale and I flew up, rented a car, and drove to Cookeville, not too far from Nashville. The show was at a movie theater in town. Charlie McCoy was there, along with the old Tex Ritter band, The Bo Weevils (Billy Sprout, Wayne Gray), Don DeWitt, PJ Babcock, and others. I did a separate show and donated my share to Snuffy and his wife. A couple of months later, Snuffy passed away. I don't reckon a day goes by that I don't think of him.

KENT WESTBERRY

We had heard about Anna Maria Island as a great vacation spot in Florida from another couple. It was only about an hour from where we were, right at Bradenton Beach. Dale and I went for a weekend on the gulf. We rented a little house that was fixed up real nice. We told Dale's sisters, Renee and Lyn, about it, and they wanted to come the next year. At first we stayed at different places. My favorite place was the Bridge Walk. It was just like the setting I had in my mind when I got the idea for "Love in the Hot Afternoon." It was a Spanish-type motel overlooking a small street with little shops lining the other side and benches, like the square I envisioned of New Orleans. You could sit on the screened-in porch and have coffee and look down from three stories up onto the street below. It had a wonderful feeling. I wrote several songs there while Dale was "asleep in the damp tangled sheets so soon," to quote my song. She usually got up about nine a.m. while on the other hand, I got up around six a.m.

Renee, Dale's sister, lives in Virginia with her husband. Richard, and Dale's sister Lyn and her daughter live in California. They all fly in and we meet once a year, along with daughter Susan and husband, Mark, daughter Judy and her daughter, Coty. Now we stay in a typical modern motel on the ocean for a family get-together.

But not Forgotten: Mom hadn't been doing so well health-wise, so we had to put her in an assisted living place. She was there for a year or so, and I went to see her every chance I got. Then suddenly I got the call, and they said she may not last throughout the day. I went down to be with her, and she passed away. Now she and my dad were both gone.

Chapter 18

STAYING BUSY

*O*ne day I was sitting around the house and wondering what I could get into when a little light went off in my head. I had a great idea. I needed to get a job to keep me from getting bored, so I contacted AARP online. I finally had a phone conversation with someone and explained that I was pretty handy at a lot of things. They set up an interview. I only wanted a part-time job. One thing led to another, and I did an interview with Catholic Charities. I got hired as a maintenance man. Right up my alley! My hours were from 6:30 a.m. to 9:30 a.m., five days a week - perfect since I'm an early riser anyway. I was finished and back home in time to have coffee with Dale each morning. The job was at the Lake Morton Senior Center, a place for older folks. Lunch was served, and they had bingo and classes of all kinds. Also, there was a little thrift store, books to read, games, and other activities.

The Eggs and I: I made all the seniors laugh with my jokes. Like the time I told them all that when Easter came, I was going to dye watermelons and hide them for the Easter egg hunt because the older folks were having a hard time seeing the eggs.

It was a great place. My job was to keep things clean and fix anything broken. That was fine for a couple of years. Then they wanted me to fill in for the management position, and that mushroomed to eight hours a day! I didn't want a full-time job, even though it included paid vacations and holidays off.

Then I met Frank. He was a homeless man who started coming by every morning as soon as I opened the doors. He'd ask me if I had any loose change I could spare, and I'd always help him out. He would also ask if he could come into the thrift store and get a pair of shoes or a shirt or something. I always let him have what he wanted. He was about six-foot-four and wore a size fifteen shoe. None in the store fit him, so he would cut the toes out of each shoe and extend the shoe with duct tape. One day I thought of something. I said, "Frank, how would you like a small job helping me set the chairs up in the other room each morning for the seniors?" There were only ten chairs. I said, "I'll give you two bucks each day." He was thrilled.

Frank was a very intelligent guy and had a college education. I asked him once why he was homeless. He replied, "Jesus was." He had me there. He said, "I like to get up and go when I want to, and go where I want to, and have no responsibilities except for myself." After about four weeks he asked me if I could give him three dollars instead of two because the cost of living had gone up. I did.

I stayed in that job four years and finally decided to turn in my resignation to have more time for writing.

In the meantime, "Funnel of Love" came out as a single by Cyndi Lauper, the rock singer, and was on her new album, *Detour*. It was also re-released by Wanda Jackson in England. At this point I'm still doing shows in and around Lakeland. One of my favorite spots was Woodall's RV Park. Charlie Duke was manager at the time and a great guy. We always had a lot of fun there. Charlie and I even went out to eat on occasion - with the wives, of course.

When we first moved to Lakeland, we tried a lot of churches and settled in at Victory Church with Pastor Blackburn. It was our church for seven years. A lot of our friends went there. It was an Assembly of God church, and he was a good pastor.

One day a neighbor told us about a church he was going to and invited us to go with him. It was also an Assembly of God church with a much smaller congregation. The pastor was Danny Applewhite, and he was on fire for the Lord. We started going there regularly because it reminded us of our church back in Tennessee. I played in the church band for a while and still sing on occasion. We've become good friends with Pastor Danny and his wife, Carol.

It was in this time period that my friend Brad passed away. Then, only five or six months later, his wife Norma also passed. We really miss them, but we know we'll see them again by and by.

Remember, it's a Business: Universal Music Publishing Group had purchased several of the publishing companies I used to write for, including Cedarwood, Sawgrass, Window Music, and Tillis Tunes. They now own the publishing to around four hundred songs of mine. This information is for current and future songwriters:

When you sign over a song for publishing to a publishing company, if the song you sign over was written before 1978 and copyrighted before that date, the publishing company has the right to the song for *twenty-eight years* with an option to renew the copyright for *another twenty-eight years*, a total of *fifty-six years*. Then the writer of the song has a right to notify the publishing company *in writing* that he or she is requesting release of the publishing of that song. It's called *"copyright recapture."* Then the writer can sell the publishing rights to someone else, or "keep publishing" for himself. For a song written, copyrighted, and signed over to a publisher *after 1978*, the copyright is only good for *thirty-five years*. Then the writer can claim it back for publishing. I sold my catalog back to Universal Music Publishing Company for the high end of five figures. I thought this might be helpful information.

Spot of Tea, Anyone? Before I close, let me share a favorite recipe with you. It's my special version for fruit tea that I always serve to company when they drop by or visit. Almost everyone seems to love it; many folks ask if I have some made. The answer is "Yes!" I always have a fresh batch in the fridge. For those interested, here's the recipe: Boil eight regular tea bags in six cups of water, add ¼-can of frozen orange juice, ¼ can of frozen apple juice, one small can of pineapple juice, ¼ cup of lemonade, four Sweet & Low packets, or four table-spoons of sugar. Mix all together in a one-gallon pitcher, then fill the rest of the pitcher with water. Stir and serve. Yum!

Aah, the Good Life: Who would have ever thought that today I would be sitting in my lanai back in Florida, in a rocking chair with my lovely wife, Dale, growing pineapples, smelling the flowers, feeding the squirrels, and counting my blessings. That's living!

Well, I reckon I've just about caught up with myself. But before I sign off, I would like to thank *everyone* who has been part of my life and my career – and that goes for the ones I didn't mention. It wasn't intentional. It's been a wonderful ride, and I thank God for being at the helm.

Now if you'll excuse me, I've got a song to write!

SONG LIST OF RECORDED SONGS
WRITTEN AND CO-WRITTEN BY KENT WESTBERRY

TITLE:	RECORDED BY:
"AIR MAIL TO HEAVEN"	CARL SMITH
"ALL THIS SHOULD MAKE YOU HAPPY"	RAY PILLOW
"AM I WHATS THE MATTER WITH YOU"	CURTIS POTTER
"AND THE ANGELS SING"	BILLY WALKER
"AS LONG AS THERE'S WOMEN LIKE YOU"	JOHNNY BUSH
"	JERRY COOPER
"BABY WHERE YOU ARE"	RANDY LEE
"BABY DOESN'T LIVE HERE ANYMORE"	ANITA ROYAL
"BACK IN SEATTLE AGAIN"	KENT WESTBERRY
"BE GLAD"	DEL REEVES
"	MIKE LANE
"	ERNEST TUBB
"	JUSTIN TUBB
"BIG OLE UGLY FOOL"	RED SOVINE
"BLUE BLUES IN GREEN"	WEBSTER BROS
"BOOGIE WITH THE DEVIL"	J.P. MAYTON .
"BRIDGE TO MEMORY LANE"	TONY BOOTH
"BUENOS NOCHES NACOGDOCHES"	BILLY WALKER
"	JOHNNY DUNCAN
"BURN YOUR BRA BABY"	ALEX HOUSTON & ELMER
"BYE BYE BUDDY"	KENT & SNUFFY
"CAMP CHUGA CHUGA"	ALEX HOUSTON & ELMER
"CHANGED MY MIND"	BILLY WALKER

133

"CHERRY BERRY WINE"	CHARLIE McCOY
"THE CARIBBEAN"	KENT WESTBERRY
"CHRISTMAS WRAPPIN'"	JERRY REED
"THE CLOSER HE GETS"	JIMMY ELLIS
"THE CLOSER SHE GETS"	MELBA MONTGOMERY
"COFFEE BROWN EYES"	BILLY WALKER
"COLD CUP OF COFFEE"	DIANA DUKE
"COWBOY"	BILLY WALKER
"CRACKERBOX MANSION"	JOSIE BROWN
"CRIME OF THE CENTURY"	KENT WESTBERRY
"THE DAYS OF YOU AND ME"	RAY PILLOW
"DIME"	BOBBY SYKES
"DON'T COME TO TEXAS"	ERNEST REY
"DON'T LET THE MORNING SUN SHINE SHAME ON YOU"	BILLY WALKER
"DRINK IT OVER"	CHARLIE LOUVIN
"EASY LADY"	KENT WESTBERRY
"	BOBBY G. RICE
"EL DIABLO"	BILLY WALKER
"EVEN ROSES HAVE THORNS"	KENT WESTBERRY
"EVERY SCHOOL BOY'S DREAM"	CORY WALKER
"FAREWELL TO ARMS"	DAVID ROGERS
"FINGERTIP FEVER"	BILL NASH
"THE FOOL I USED TO BE"	SAMMY DAVIS JR.
"	CARL PERKINS
"FOREVER YOURS"	BUCK OWENS
"	TONY BOOTH
"FORGET THERE EVER WAS A YESTERDAY"	KENT WESTBERRY

	& DALE TURNER
"FREJOLES" (INSTRUMENTAL)	THE CHAMPS
"FUNNEL OF LOVE"	WANDA JACKSON
"	THE CRAMPS
"	CYNDI LAUPER
"	TERRAPLANE SUN
"	SQURL
"	MARTI BROM
"	ROSIE FLORES
"	MARSHMELLOWS
"	NIKKI LANE
"GOD COUNTRY APPLE PIE WILLEX AND YOU"	KENT WESTBERRY
"GOIN QUIETLY CRAZY"	MELBA MONTGOMERY
"GROWIN OLD WITH GRACE"	MAX D. BARNES
"GUESS WE THOUGHT THE WORLD WOULD END"	BOBBY HELMS
"HALF PAST LONESOME"	LORENA PRATER
"HANDLE WITH CARE"	LITTLE JIMMY DICKENS
"HAPPY HONKIN HONKY TONKIN TRUCK DRIVIN MAN"	DALE TURNER
"HELLO OUT THERE"	CARL BELEW
"	NICK NOBLE
"	DARRELL McCALL
"HELP ME UP, DARLIN"	WILLIE SAMPLES
"HELPLESS HOPELESS FOOL"	MEL TILLIS
"HERE COMES PETER COTTON CLAUS"	ALEX HOUSTON & ELMER
"HEY PINNOCH"	THE HARDIN TRIO
"HIGH COST OF GIVING"	KENT WESTBERRY
"HOMETOWN GIRL"	JAN CRUTCHFIELD

"HOORAY FOR ME"	MARTI BROWN
"HOW'D YA LIKE TO TAKE A GOOD TIME HOME TONIGHT"	RAY PILLOW
"I'M A BLUEBIRD"	HAROLD MORRISON
"I BELIEVE IN JESUS"	KENT WESTBERRY
"I CAN FEEL HIM TOUCHING YOU (ALL OVER ME)"	HARLAN SANDERS
"	JOHNNY BUSH
"I CAN'T CLIMB THIS MOUNTAIN ALONE"	JANEY GLENCLOSE
"I DON'T NEED YOU ANYMORE"	ANITA CARTER
"I DON'T THINK I'D BELIEVE YOU"	AFARON YOUNG
"I FINALLY GAVE HER ENOUGH ROPE TO HANG"	BUCK OWENS
"I JUST DON'T KNOW HOW TO SAY NO"	FARON YOUNG
"I JUST DON'T UNDERSTAND"	ANN-MARGRET
"	THE BEATLES
"	JERRY REED
"	LES PAUL & MARY FORD
"	FREDDY & THE DREAMERS
"	VICKY LAWRENCE
"	RAY ELLIS & HIS ORCHESTRA
"	SPOON
"	JOE SUN
"I JUST WENT OUT OF STYLE"	LAURA SUE YORK
"I'LL FORGET YOU THE MINUTE I DIE"	JERRY COOPER
"I'M GONNA BE GONE"	JIMMY DEAN
"I'M GONNA RISE"	BILLY WALKER
"I'M MISSING ME WITH YOU"	GRANT TINGEY

I'VE GOT A SONG TO WRITE

"I SENT YOU ME"	KENT WESTBERRY
"I'VE GOT YESTERDAY"	KITTY WELLS
"	BILL PHILLIPS
"IF HEARTACHES WERE WINE"	STONEWALL JACKSON
"	JERRY BURKE
"IF IT'S THE LAST FLING I DO"	GARY LINK
"IF THE WHOLE WORLD WAS AN ASH TRAY"	KENT WESTBERRY
"IF YOU HAD ONLY TAKEN THE TIME"	CHARLIE PRIDE
"	JOHNNY PAYCHECK
"IT'S ME THAT HURTS THE MOST"	LITTLE JIMMY DICKENS
"IT DIDN'T TAKE THE BLUES LONG"	DON LEWIS
"JUST TWO STRANGERS PASSING IN THE NIGHT"	MEL TILLIS & SHERRY BRYCE
"LET ME BE THE ONE YOU LOVE"	MARK STEWART
"LET ME LOVE THE LEAVIN FROM YOUR MIND"	FARON YOUNG
"LET'S PUT CHRIST BACK IN CHRISTMAS"	STONEMANS
"LITTLE BIT OF HEAVEN"	EARL SINKS
"LITTLE EVIL"	STAN DEE
"LITTLE JACK DANIEL"	LITTLE JIMMY DICKENS
"LONG TIME DRIFTER"	KENT WESTBERRY
"LOOK WHAT THE WIND BLEW IN"	JAN BEARD
"LOSING YOU JUST DAWNED ON ME TODAY"	TONY BOOTH
"LOUISIANA LOVE"	JIMMY C. NEWMAN
"LOVE AND NOT THE NAILS"	BILLY WALKER
"LOVE AT THE LAUNDRYMAT"	KENT WESTBERRY
"LOVE IN THE HOT AFTERNOON"	GENE WATSON
"	JIM ED BROWN
"	VICKY LAWRENCE

"	MARK CHESTNUT
"	WAYLON JENNINGS
"LOVE IS SO LIKE A FINE VINTAGE WINE"	MERVIN SHINER
"LOVE FOR BREAKFAST"	KENT WESTBERRY
	& DALE TURNER
"LOVE ME"	EDDY ARNOLD
"LOVE RINGS AN OLD BELL WITH ME"	DALE TURNER
"LOVELAND"	BILLY GRAMMAR
"LOVIN' STUFF"	JIMMY VOYTEK
"MARRIED TO A JUKEBOX"	KENT WESTBERRY
"MARY GOES ROUND"	BOBBY HELMS
"	KENT WESTBERRY
"	MERV SHINER
"MEMORY MAKER"	MEL TILLIS
	KENT WESTBERRY
"MEXICALI MOON"	BILLY WALKER
"MR. RIGHT AND MRS. WRONG"	KENT WESTBERRY
	& DALE TURNER
"	MEL TILLIS & SHERRY BRYCE
"	LANDON DODD
	& AMBER DIGBY
"A MONKEY OUT OF ME"	DAVE NICELY
"MY BABY DON'T ROCK ME NOW"	KENT WESTBERRY
"NEONS"	STONEWALL JACKSON
"THE NIGHT BEFORE THE DAY"	KENT WESTBERRY
"NO LAUGHING MATTER"	KENT WESTBERRY
"NO PLACE TO PARK"	KENT WESTBERRY

"OF ALL THE THINGS YOU LEFT"	JIMMY NEWMAN
"OLD HABITS"	KENT WESTBERRY
"ONE MORE DAY"	KENT WESTBERRY
"ONE TOO MANY MEMORIES"	RAY PILLOW
"	CURTIS POTTER
"PARTY PEOPLE"	HANK WILLIAMS JR.
	& LOIS JOHNSON
"PICTURES"	MEL TILLIS
"PLAY ME A LEAVIN SONG"	KENT WESTBERRY
"POWER OF THE NEON"	JIM KANDY
"PRETEND YOU'RE STILL MINE"	THE SHEPPARDS
"	THE ZIPPERS
"REACHING FOR HER, LEANING ON ME"	SUSAN RAYE
"RIGHT AS RAIN"	WANDA CONKLIN
"RODEO GIRL"	LYNN & PRISCILLA FULCHER
"SAME OLD SONG AND DANCE"	DALE TURNER
"SATURDAY NIGHT LIVE"	BILL NASH
"SEE THAT LIGHT ON YONDER MOUNTAIN"	THE GREENES
"	CHUCK WAGON GANG
"SHADY SIDE OF CHARLOTTE"	NAT STUCKEY
"SHE COMES TO ME"	MERV SHINER
"SHE GETS TO ME"	KENT WESTBERRY
"SHE'S A HEARTACHE IN HIGH HEEL SHOES"	BILLY WALKER
"SHE'S COME BACK"	GENE MCDANIELS
"SHE SIMPLY LEFT"	MAC WISEMAN
"SHE WON'T LET ME FORGET HER"	BOB WILLS
"	JODY NIX

"SIDE STREET"	DIANA DUKE
"SLOW MOTION"	FREDDY WELLER
"SNIFF SNIFF BOO HOO HOO HOO"	DALE TURNER
"SOFTEST TOUCH IN TOWN"	BOBBY G. RICE
"SOMEONE LEFT THE LIGHT ON IN YOUR EYES"	BILLY WALKER
"SORROWS TEARING DOWN THE HOUSE"	LITTLE JIMMY DICKENS
"	PORTER WAGONER
	& DOLLY PARTON
"	PORTER WAGONER
	& SKEETER DAVIS
"	STONEWALL JACKSON
"	DAVE NICELY
"SPIT IN THE DEVILS EYE"	KENT WESTBERRY
"STANDING BY"	RAY PILLOW
"THE STAR OF THE SHOW"	RED SOVINE
"	CARL PERKINS
"SWEET SPANISH MEMORIES"	BILLY WALKER
"TEARS, TEARS, TEARS"	BETTY ROGERS
"THANK YOU FOR BEING YOU"	MEL TILLIS
"THAT OLD EL PASO STORY AGAIN"	BILLY WALKER
"THAT'S HOW HIGH A MAN CAN GO"	FREDDIE HART
"	BOBBY LEWIS
"THAT'S NO SIGN"	DIANA DUKE
"THAT'S WHERE LONESOME LIVES"	OBREY WILSON
"THAT'S WHERE THE HURT COMES IN"	MEL TILLIS
"THAT'S WHY"	DANTE
"THEM BOOZE DRINKIN BUDDIES OF MINE"	HARLAN SANDERS

"THERE'S ONE MEMORY I'D LIKE TO MEET AGAIN"	RAY PILLOW
"THREE FINGERS OF TEQUILA"	KENT WESTBERRY
"THREE LITTLE MEMORIES"	DALE TURNER
"TIME HAVE MERCY ON ME"	DIANA DUKE
"TOGETHER SEPERATELY"	DIANA DUKE
"TOGETHER TONIGHT"	RAY PILLOW
"TWO PEOPLE PARTY"	KEVIN & JULIE
"TWO'S"	SHERRY CARLISLE
"UNDERLOVED AND OVERLONELY"	LYN CHILDRESS
"	KATY MOFFITT
"WANDA RIDES A HONDA"	CORY WALKER
"WATCHING ELIZABETH PLAY"	JOHNNY DUNCAN
"WE'D DESTROY EACH OTHER"	CARL & PEARL BUTLER
"WE GOTTA GET AWAY FROM IT ALL"	TOM GRANT
"WE'RE AS CLOSE AS WE CAN GET TO BEING GONE"	THE RAMONDOS
"WE'VE GOT TO START MEETING LIKE THIS"	JERRY WEST
"WHAT ABOUT TOMORROW"	KAREN WHEELER
"WHAT WE USED TO HANG ON TO IS GONE"	HANK WILLIAMS JR.
	& LOIS JOHNSON
"	DICKEY LEE
"WHO'S CHEATING WHO"	PRICILLA MITCHELL
"WHO'S SHOES ARE THESE"	BILLY WALKER
"WHY DO I KEEP DOING THIS TO US"	CARL SMITH
"THE WRONG GENERATION"	CARL BUTLER
"WILD TEXAS ROSE"	BILLY WALKER
"WINDS OF CHANGE"	GENE WATSON
"	JOHNNY BUSH

"WOE IS ME"	JERRY WOODARD
"WOMAN MADE MAN"	DALE WARD
"YOU ARE THE ONE"	MEL TILLIS &
	SHERRY BRYCE
"	KENT WESTERRY
	& DALE TURNER
"YOU BROKE MY LITTLE WOODEN HEART"	ALEX HOUSTON & ELMER
"YOU DO SOMETHING SPECIAL TO ME"	PRICE MITCHELL
"YOU DON'T TREAT ME RIGHT"	FARON YOUNG
"	MARIA DALLAS
"YOU KISS ME LIKE YOU'RE GLAD TO SEE ME GO"	JIM KANDY
"YOU'LL KNOW HOW IT FEELS TO BE ME"	KENT WESTBERRY
"YOUR MEMORY WALKS THROUGH WALLS"	FREDDY WELLER
"	BRAD CASWELL
"	DAMON GRAY
"YOU'RE NOT REALLY LEAVING ME ARE YOU?"	RUBY WRIGHT